The Amazing Outdoor Activity Book

ANGELA WILKES

DK

A DK Publishing Book

*For Heather and But, in memory
of all our childhood expeditions.*

Designer Jane Bull
Photographer Dave King

Project Editor Stella Love
Managing Editor Jane Yorke
Senior Art Editor Chris Scollen
US Editor Camela Decaire
Production Josie Alabaster

First American Edition, 1996
6 8 10 9 7 5

Published in the United States by
DK Publishing, Inc.
375 Hudson Street New York, New York 10014

ISBN 0-7894-0467-2
A CIP catalog record is available from the Library of Congress.

Color reproduction by Bright Arts, Hong Kong
Printed and bound in Spain by Artes Gráficas Toledo, S.A.U.
D.L. TO: 751-2004

Dorling Kindersley would like to thank Mandy Earey for invaluable
design assistance, Chris Branfield for jacket design, Joanne Downey for text
fitting, Helen Drew and Carey Combe for editorial help, Cathy Mann for food
preparation, and Stephen Bull. Dorling Kindersley would also like to thank the
following models for appearing in this book: Holly Cowgill, Kelly Gomeze,
Emma Judson, Lawrence King, Jade Ogugua, Sam Priddy, Tebergé
Ricketts, Tim Shaw, and Darren Singh. The project models were
made by Jane Bull and Angela Wilkes.

CONTENTS

COLLECTIONS

OUTDOOR LIVING

TRACKING AND TRAILING

 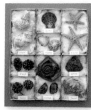 

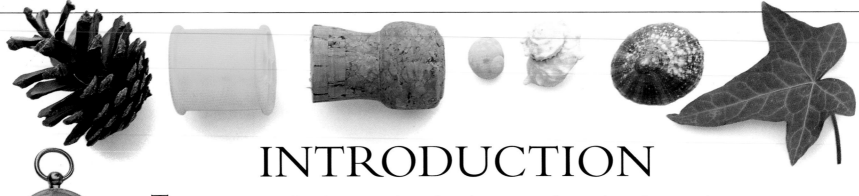

INTRODUCTION

This book is full of great ideas for things to do and make outdoors all year round. As well as being fun, many of the projects will help you find out all kinds of fascinating things about the natural world. Read through the activities and decide which one you want to try, then start collecting useful materials. When you finish a project, remember to put away all your equipment and to clean up any mess.

Equipment and materials to collect

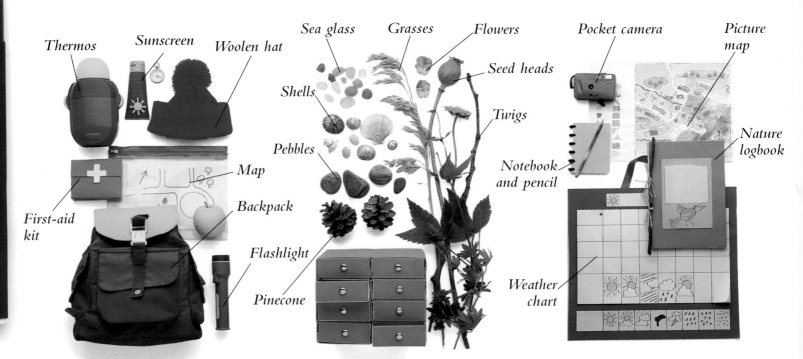

Thermos · Sunscreen · Woolen hat
Sea glass · Grasses · Flowers
Seed heads
Shells
Pebbles
Twigs
Map
First-aid kit
Backpack
Flashlight
Pinecone
Pocket camera · Picture map
Notebook and pencil
Nature logbook
Weather chart

Outdoor living
It is important to be properly equipped for expeditions and trips. These are some of the items you should always take with you.

Nature collections
Collecting things you find outdoors provides a good starting point for learning about nature. This book gives you ideas for what to collect and how to display it.

Keeping records
You can learn a lot by recording your observations. Find out how to draw maps, keep a logbook, and make your own weather chart.

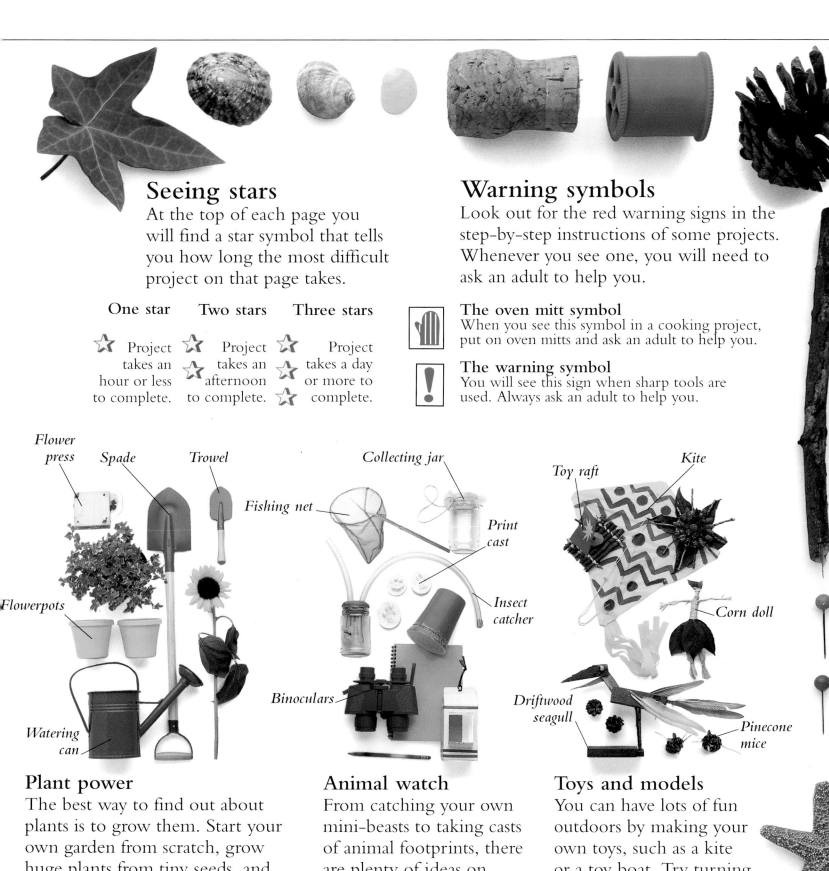

Seeing stars

At the top of each page you will find a star symbol that tells you how long the most difficult project on that page takes.

One star

☆ Project takes an hour or less to complete.

Two stars

☆☆ Project takes an afternoon to complete.

Three stars

☆☆☆ Project takes a day or more to complete.

Warning symbols

Look out for the red warning signs in the step-by-step instructions of some projects. Whenever you see one, you will need to ask an adult to help you.

The oven mitt symbol
When you see this symbol in a cooking project, put on oven mitts and ask an adult to help you.

The warning symbol
You will see this sign when sharp tools are used. Always ask an adult to help you.

Flower press   *Spade*   *Trowel*

Collecting jar

Fishing net

Print cast

Flowerpots

Insect catcher

Watering can

Binoculars

Toy raft   *Kite*

Corn doll

Driftwood seagull

Pinecone mice

Plant power

The best way to find out about plants is to grow them. Start your own garden from scratch, grow huge plants from tiny seeds, and press your own flowers.

Animal watch

From catching your own mini-beasts to taking casts of animal footprints, there are plenty of ideas on how to attract and then study wildlife.

Toys and models

You can have lots of fun outdoors by making your own toys, such as a kite or a toy boat. Try turning natural materials into unusual models, too.

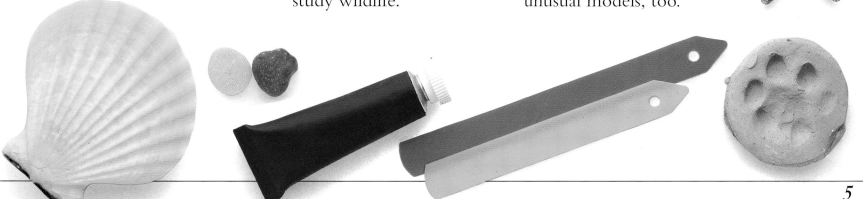

OUTDOOR SURVIVAL KIT

Exploring the great outdoors is exciting, but it is important that you are properly prepared before you go. Wear comfortable clothes and shoes and pack everything else you need, such as food, maps, and a waterproof jacket, in a backpack. Here are all the essential items you will need, together with ideas for things you might find useful for some nature detective work.

Being prepared

Plan your route before you go and listen to the weather forecast in the morning so that you know what to wear and what to take with you.

Cap with visor

Headgear

A woolly hat will keep your head warm in cold weather. When it is hot, a cap with a visor will keep the sun out of your eyes.

Woolly hat

Pocket compass

Waterproof jacket

Finding the way

Take a map and a compass to help you find your way. Be sure to let your parents know where you are going and how long you expect to be out.

Backpack

The best backpacks have lots of useful pockets.

Money belt

A money belt is useful for keeping coins and small items handy.

Maps and plastic case

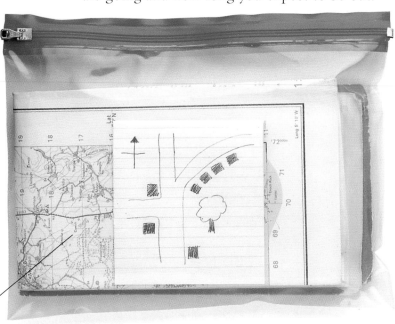

A plastic case will keep your maps dry.

What to take

Here are some suggestions for things to carry. Some are essential, such as food and drink, some will help you in case of an accident, and others will help you study things that you see.

Candy and chocolate will give you energy.

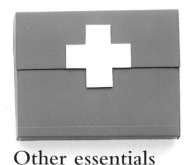

First-aid kit

Take some water or juice to drink.

Plastic lunch box

Thermos

Supplies

If you are going out for longer than half a day, you will need food and drink to keep you going.

Other essentials

A first-aid kit, sunscreen, tissues, money, and a flashlight are all important items to take with you.

Protect your skin on sunny days.

Sunscreen

Tissues

Flashlight

Carry coins and useful phone numbers in a small wallet in case you need to phone for help.

Wallet

Nature spotting

When you are out walking, you may want to make notes and sketches of insects, flowers, and birds, or collect interesting finds. The items shown here will help you.

Notebook and pencil

Binoculars

Take a small camera with you in case you see anything unusual.

Camera

Plastic bags and containers

Bug bottle

Pocket magnifying glass

Length of string

Carry some containers for collecting specimens.

Pocketknife

7

UNDER COVER

Being able to build a simple shelter is a useful survival skill, but it is also simply fun to do in your own yard. You can make a tepee from bamboo poles and a piece of material. Or why not make a portable blind so you can watch animals from close-up without them seeing you? It is easier to make both projects if you have a friend with you. Turn the page to see the finished tepee and blind.

EQUIPMENT

Ruler

Scissors

Felt-tip pen

2-in (5-cm) paintbrush

Jars of water

You will need

For the blind

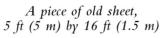

5 lengths of bamboo, 2 ft (60 cm) long

A piece of old sheet, 4½ ft (1.35 m) by 3 ft (96 cm)

String

A piece of old sheet, 5 ft (5 m) by 16 ft (1.5 m)

For the tepee

5 lengths of bamboo, 2ft (60 cm) long

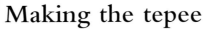

1 length of bamboo, 17 in (45 cm) long

String

Making the tepee

Large, strong rubber bands

Poster paint or fabric paint

6 lengths of bamboo, 6½ ft (2 m) long

1 Stand the six bamboo poles together so the tops meet. Wrap rubber bands around them 15 in (38 cm) from the top to make a frame.

2 Ask a friend to hold the standing poles steady at the top and splay them out until they are nearly 3 ft (84 cm) apart at the bottom, as shown.

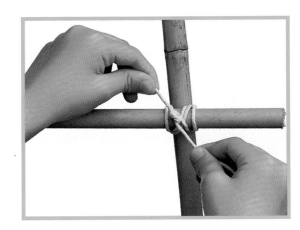

3   Use string to tie each of the five 2-ft (60-cm) poles to a long pole so they cross. Wind the string around the poles and tie a reef knot.★

4   Position the five 2-ft (60-cm) poles about 2 ft (60 cm) up from the bottom of each of the long poles, as shown. Leave a space for the door.

5   Tie the 17-in (45-cm) pole across the last two long poles about 3 ft (85 cm) down from the rubber bands to make the door frame of the tepee.

6   Ask a friend to hold the fabric half over the door of the tepee. Wrap the fabric around the poles so the two ends meet at the door.

7   Bunch the fabric in where the poles are tied together at the top. Wind a piece of string tightly around the fabric and tie a reef knot.

8   Pull the fabric down each pole. Cut two holes in the fabric on either side of each pole. Then tie string through them and around the poles.

9   Tie the fabric to the poles in the same way where the shorter poles are tied to the long poles and at the top of each side of the door.

10   Mix paint and water in jars and use a large paintbrush to paint the tepee fabric with bold shapes, such as circles and crosses.

11   Paint a decorative border along the bottom and around the door opening to complete the tepee design.

★ *See page 62.*

SIMPLE SHELTERS

Making the blind

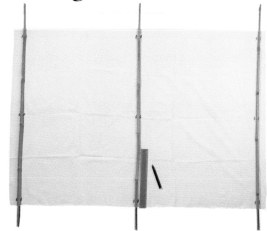

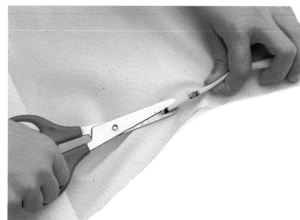

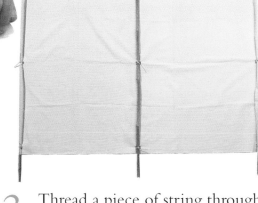

1 Spread out fabric for the blind flat on the ground. Lay the three poles across it as shown, with one at each end and one in the middle.

2 With a pen, make marks on both sides of each pole near the top, the bottom, and in the center. Then cut a small hole on each mark.

3 Thread a piece of string through each set of holes and around the pole between them. Then knot the strings to fix the fabric to the poles.

Invisible observers

From behind your blind you can watch wildlife. Take a blanket to sit on and have your binoculars and notepad handy. Remember to be as quiet as you possibly can.

Heading home
To take the blind home, pull it out of the ground, fold it in half along the center pole and roll it up.

Make sure the slits are big enough for your binoculars.

Setting up
To set up the blind, stretch it out to its full width and push each pole into the ground. If the ground is hard, ask an adult to help you. The blind is big enough to conceal two people. You can paint your blind green and brown to camouflage it.

Closed tepee

When the door of the tepee is closed, the two ends of the fabric should meet halfway across the opening. The tepee is not waterproof, so remember to put it away at night or if it rains.

4 Draw two rectangular slits on the fabric halfway between the center and each outer pole and 10 in (25 cm) down from the top. Cut out the slits.

Setting up camp

Choose a flat, dry place to set up your tepee and then splay out the poles until the fabric is fairly taut. Put a blanket inside to make it cozy and stock it with the supplies you need.

You can copy these decorations for your tepee or try out ideas of your own.

Fold the fabric flaps back around the door poles when you want the door open.

FOOD AND SUPPLIES

Whether you are going on a day's hike, a secret expedition, or just to the park, you will get hungry! What food you take will be limited by how you are going to carry it, but every picnic has the same basic elements. Include something filling, something sweet, a drink, and treats to nibble.

Fillers
Make a roll or sandwich the main part of your picnic and fill it with your favorite things. Try not to overfill it so it will be easy to eat, and wrap it in foil or plastic wrap to keep it fresh.

Tuna, mayonnaise, and cucumber roll

Roll filled with salami, sliced cheese, lettuce, and tomato

Pita bread stuffed with salami, sliced cucumber, and tomato

French roll filled with sliced ham, lettuce, and tomato

Sweet things
Cookies and small pieces of cake are good for picnics and do not take up much room in your pack. Take more than you think you need and add some pieces of fresh fruit.

Chocolate brownies

Cookies

Apple

Bunches of grapes

Pear

Tangerine

Extras

If you are going on a special picnic, you could take along some salad or vegetable sticks in small containers, and small individually wrapped cheeses.

Carrot, pepper, and cucumber sticks

Thirst quenchers

Take as much to drink as you can carry. Water and fruit juice are more refreshing than sodas. In cold weather you could take a hot drink or soup in a thermos. Make sure you screw on the lids of drinks tightly.

Water bottle filled with fruit juice

Different small cheeses

Small thermos for cold or hot drinks, or soup

Quick snacks and nibbles

It is a good idea to pack a few snacks and treats. Put them in one of the pockets of your backpack. Remember to collect any wrappers to throw away at home.

Chips

Nuts and raisins

Candy

Chocolate bars

Packing your supplies

If you are going on a hike, you will need to pack your food in a small lunch box and put it in your backpack. For a picnic you could use a picnic basket or cooler. Why not make a simple bundle for a picnic in the park?

Small picnic basket

Picnic bundle on a stick

FIRESIDE COOKING

What simpler way to cook than to wrap your food in foil and bake it in your campfire? Use aluminum foil to wrap the food, folding in the edges tightly. Wait until the flames die down, then ask an adult to help you push the packages into the glowing embers. Here you can find out how to bake potato surprises, apples, and garlic-and-herb bread in foil. These recipes each make one serving.

EQUIPMENT

Cutting board *Grater* *Sharp knife* *Apple corer* *Teaspoon*

Aluminum foil *Small bowl*

You will need

For the potato surprise

1 large potato *Ham cut in cubes* *1 chopped tomato* *Grated cheese*

For the baked apple

1 large dessert apple *A handful of raisins* *1 teaspoon brown sugar* *2 tablespoons butter*

For the garlic-and-herb bread

1 French roll *¼ cup (2 oz/55 g) cream cheese* *Chives* *Parsley* *¼ teaspoon salt* *1 clove of garlic*

Potato surprise

Garlic-and-herb bread

1 Slice a lid off the potato and scoop out the inside with the apple corer. Fill the hollow with the chopped ham, tomato, and cheese.

2 Put the lid back on the potato and wrap it in foil. Bake it for 1 to 1½ hours until it is soft in the center and cooked through.

1 Chop the parsley, chives, and garlic. Mix the salt and herbs into the cream cheese with a spoon until the mixture is soft.

2 Make cuts along the bread and spread the cheese mixture inside them. Wrap the foil around the bread and bake it for 15 minutes.

Baked apple

1 Lay the apple on two overlapping squares of foil. Core the apple and fill the hole with raisins. Spoon some brown sugar on top.

2 Put the butter on top of the sugar and wrap the apple in both layers of foil. Then bake it for 30 to 40 minutes, until it is soft.

An outdoor feast

Ask an adult to take the foil packages out of the fire for you. Let them cool slightly and then unwrap them. Test the potato and apple with a sharp knife to make sure they are soft. If not, wrap them up again and put them back in the embers to cook longer.

Baked apple

Potato surprise

Serve the foil packages in napkins so no one burns their fingers.

Because you are outside, use plastic spoons to eat your potato and apple.

Use two layers of foil for baked apples to protect the apple skin from burning.

Garlic-and-herb bread

BARBECUING

Food grilled outdoors on a barbecue has a special smoky flavor all its own. Even the simplest things taste delicious. Here you can find out how to barbecue sausage kabobs and hamburgers. Prepare the food indoors, then take it out to the barbecue to be cooked. Make sure there is an adult there to help you. The recipes here will serve four people.

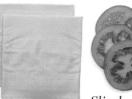

EQUIPMENT

Fork

Sharp knife

Mixing bowl

Spatula

Cutting board

4 skewers

You will need

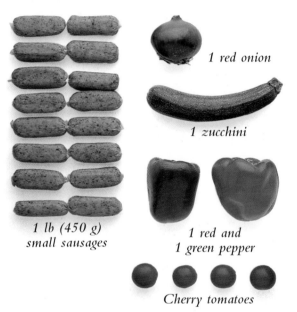

For the kabobs

1 red onion

1 zucchini

1 red and
1 green pepper

1 lb (450 g)
small sausages

Cherry tomatoes

For the hamburgers

1 lb (450 g) ground beef

4 hamburger
buns

1 egg
yolk

$^{1}/_{2}$ an onion,
finely chopped

Salt and
pepper

For garnishing

Sliced cheese

Sliced
tomato

Sliced cucumber

Lettuce

Making the kabobs

1 Remove the cores and pith from the peppers and cut them into squares. Slice the zucchini into rounds, and cut the peeled onion into quarters.

2 Push the chopped vegetables and sausages onto the skewers as shown. Be very careful with the sharp points on the skewers.

3 Ask an adult to check when the barbecue is ready. Then grill the kabobs for 10 to 15 minutes, turning them so that they cook on all sides.

Making the hamburgers

1 Put the ground beef, egg yolk, finely chopped onion, and salt and pepper into the mixing bowl. Mix them together well with one hand.

2 Split the mixture into four even-sized parts. Roll each one into a ball, then flatten it and round the edges to make a circular hamburger.

3 When the barbecue is hot, put the hamburgers on the grill and cook them for 5 to 10 minutes on each side, until they are firm and brown.

The outdoor grill

You can eat the kabobs immediately. Carefully pick up the hot skewers, then slide the sausages and vegetables off onto your plate, using a fork. Assemble the hamburgers as shown below for a real feast!

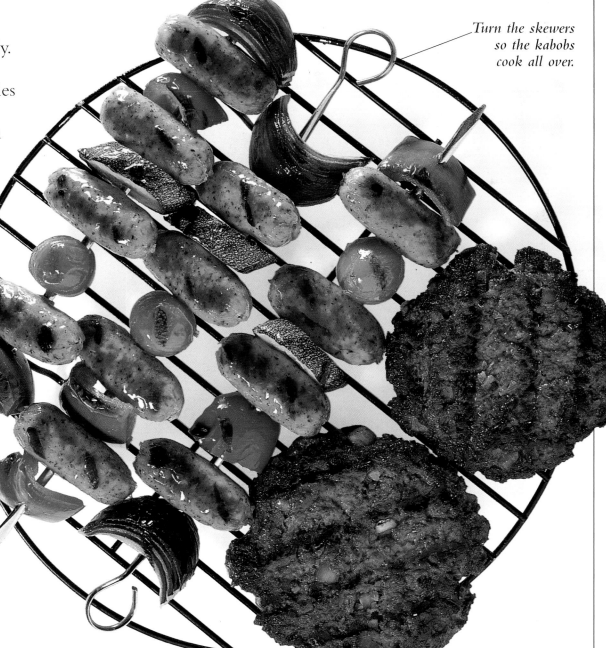

Turn the skewers so the kabobs cook all over.

All in a bun
Arrange each hamburger in a bun with a slice of cheese, sliced tomato, cucumber, and some crisp lettuce.

Other kabobs
You can vary your kabobs by using cubes of chicken or another meat.

17

ANIMAL TRACKS

You can keep a permanent record of animal prints you come across outside by making casts of them from plaster of paris. If you can't find clear animal tracks, why not start by making casts of hand- and footprints you have made yourself? You can put the clear casts into your nature museum.

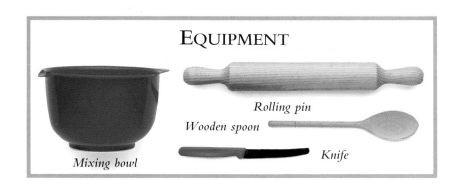

EQUIPMENT

Rolling pin

Wooden spoon

Knife

Mixing bowl

You will need

(For one large plaster cast)

Self-hardening modeling clay, if you are making your own prints★

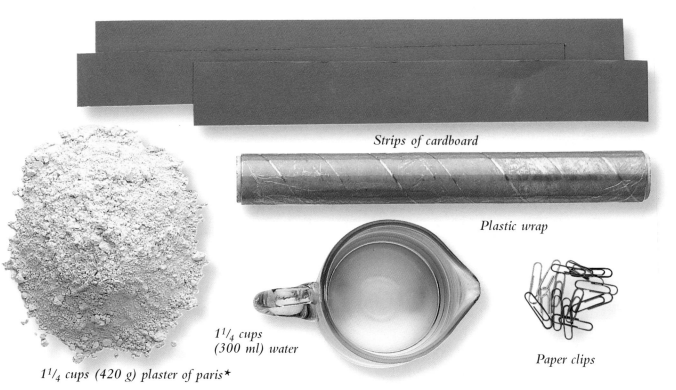

Strips of cardboard

Plastic wrap

$1^1/_4$ cups (300 ml) water

1¼ cups (420 g) plaster of paris★

Paper clips

Making a print

1 Lay plastic wrap on your work surface. Cut a lump of clay and place it on the plastic wrap, then roll it out until it is about $1/_2$ in (1 cm) thick.

2 Press your hand, foot, or shoe firmly down onto the clay to make a clear print, then lift it off again carefully.

Making a cast

1 Bend a strip of cardboard into a circle big enough to go around the print. Clip the ends together and push it into the clay around the print.

2 Put the plaster of paris in the mixing bowl and pour in the water. Mix them with your wooden spoon until smooth and runny.

3 Pour the plaster mixture into the cardboard ring until it is about 1 in (2.5 cm) deep. Leave for about 15 minutes, until the plaster has set hard.

4 Unclip the cardboard and peel it off the plaster. Gently ease the fragile plaster cast away from the clay mold. Leave the cast to set for a day.

Animal casts

You can take casts of animal tracks outdoors in the same way. Just push a cardboard ring into the mud or sand around each print, and then follow the instructions for making a cast.

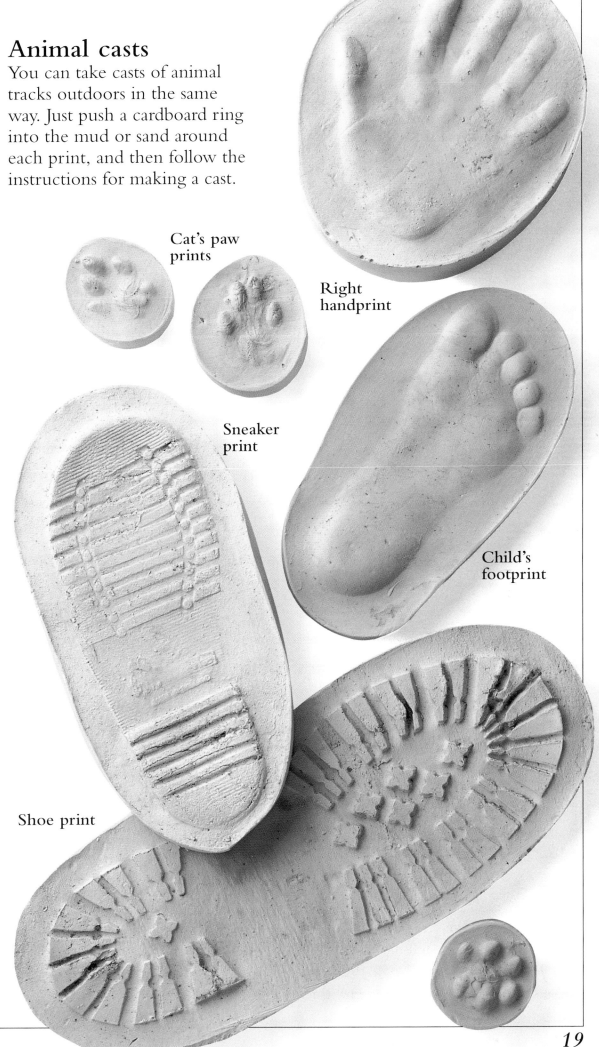

Cat's paw prints

Right handprint

Sneaker print

Child's footprint

Shoe print

ON THE TRAIL

Tracking skills can be really useful for finding your way around. Here you can find out how to lay and follow a trail using different materials. Choose things that will show up on the ground and collect enough for a whole trail. Then you can have fun with your friends laying a simple trail, or inventing one with coded signs to follow.

A trail code

You will need a friend to lay a trail for you to follow. If you use a coded trail, you must both agree what the signs mean and keep a record of them in your notebook. Here are some useful signs made with sticks, stones, and leaves.

You will need

(Any one of the following things)

Evergreen or brightly colored leaves

Strips of old fabric

Stones and pebbles

A notebook to record your trail code

Small straight twigs

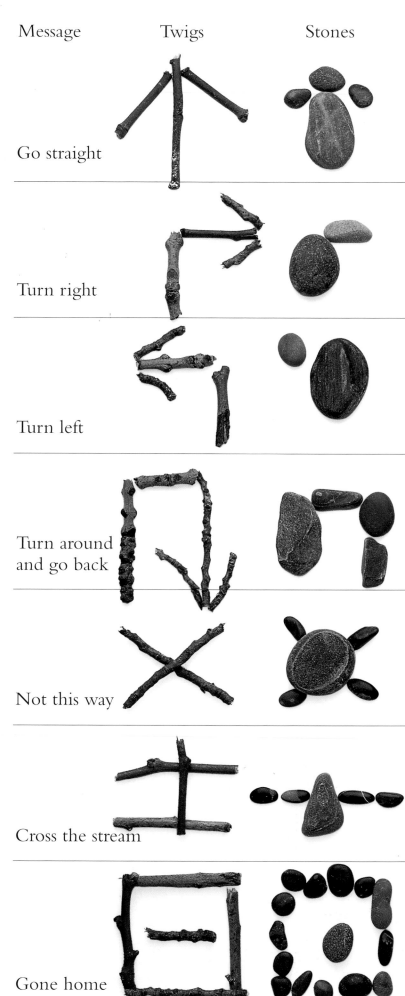

Message	Twigs	Stones
Go straight		
Turn right		
Turn left		
Turn around and go back		
Not this way		
Cross the stream		
Gone home		

Leaves

Plain trails

You do not have to lay a coded trail. You could make simple direction arrows on the ground with leaves, twigs, or stones.

Telltale signs

You could tie strips of fabric to bushes or low-lying branches to show which way to go. Remember to remove them all and take them home afterward.

Direction arrow made from pebbles

Trail game

Why not play a trail game? You will need at least two people to lay and follow a trail, but it is more fun if there are four of you so that you can work together in pairs. Two of you lay the trail and the other two have to see if they can follow it all the way to the end.

Before you start, figure out your trail code together so that you all know what the signs mean. Give the trail layers a ten minute headstart or, if the trail is going to be around a yard, let them finish laying it on the ground before the trackers set off.

Laying the trail

Always lay the signs on the same side of the path, and place them where they show up. Space them about 15 feet (five meters) apart so that the trackers do not have too far to go between each one.

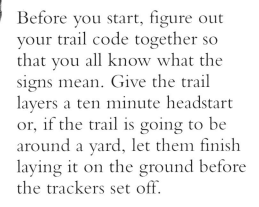

Make sure you lay the signs very clearly at any tricky spots, such as at a path fork, or where grass undergrowth is long.

Direction arrow made from leaves

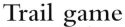

MAKING A MAP

Being able to find your way around is a vital outdoor skill, and you will find it useful to know how to follow or draw a simple map. A map is a bird's-eye view of an area. It shows you the way to go from one place to another, what the land looks like, and where things are. Here and on the next three pages you can find out how to draw a route map, a picture map, and a treasure map.

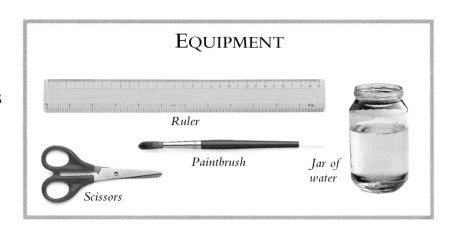

EQUIPMENT

Ruler

Paintbrush

Jar of water

Scissors

You will need

Pocket compass

Thick paper

Poster paints (or colored pencils or crayons)

A fine felt-tip pen

Notebook and pencil

Simple route map

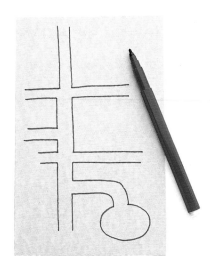

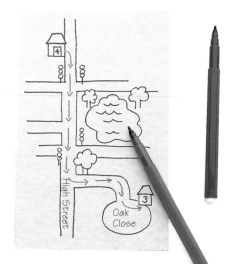

1 Start by drawing the main roads between your home and a friend's. Show where the smaller side roads join on to them.

2 Draw in the two houses or buildings at each end of the route and add any helpful landmarks, such as traffic lights, trees, or a pond.

3 Write on the street numbers of the two homes and the names of the most important roads. Then draw arrows to show the best route to follow.

Picture map

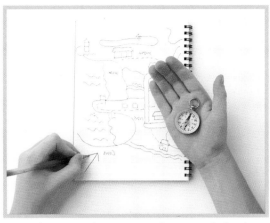

1 Find a spot outdoors with a good view of your chosen area and make a sketch in your notebook, showing all the main landmarks.

2 Stay in the same place and find out which way is North with your pocket compass.★ Draw an arrow on your map pointing in that direction.

3 Back home, turn the sketch so that the North arrow points straight up and copy the map in this position onto a sheet of paper.

Creating a map key

Most maps use picture symbols to give you information about the area and in one corner there is usually a "key" to tell you what the pictures mean. Make a list of the things you want to show on your map and draw a symbol to represent each one.

Here are some symbols for the sort of things you might want to put on a map of a seaside town.

Steep hill · Pebble beach · Road · Mailbox

Farmland · Cliff · Church · Hotel

River · Coniferous forest · Ice-cream stand · Lighthouse

Sea · Deciduous forest · Café · Bus stop

Sandy beach · Footpath · Telephone booth · Viewing point

Filling in the details

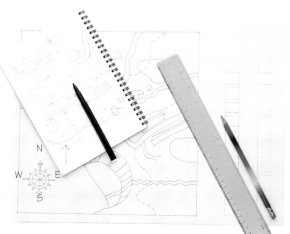

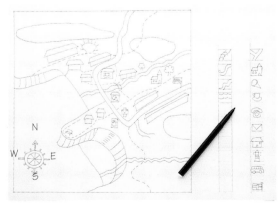

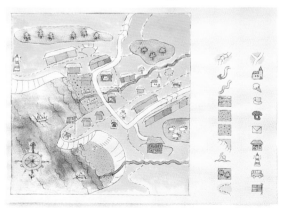

4 In one corner of the map, mark in the points of the compass. Draw boxes for the key picture symbols at one side of the map.

5 Still using your sketch as a reference, draw the picture symbols in place on the map itself and in the boxes for the key.

6 Color in your map making sure the symbols match those in the key. Then add place names to the map and label the key symbols.

FINDING THE WAY

A finished route map shows the quickest route between two places. A picture map will also help you find your way around, but it gives other information as well, as does the treasure map. To follow a map, turn it so that the symbols on it, especially the paths or roads, line up with what you see in front of you. Then you are ready to set off!

Route map

If someone asks you the way, it is often better to draw a quick map than to try to give directions. Practice drawing route maps to interesting places in your area.

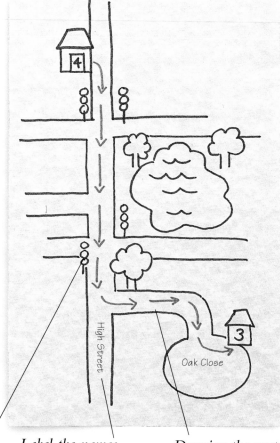

Traffic lights are good landmarks in towns. Make sure you put them in the right place on the map.

Label the names of the main roads to follow on your map.

Drawing the route in a different color helps make it clearer.

Picture map

A picture map of a favorite place or a vacation destination is a great record of where you have been, as well as a wonderful picture.

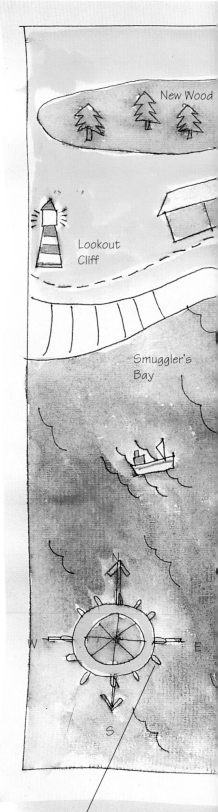

Make the compass decorative if you wish. This one is based on a ship's wheel.

Treasure map

Why not make up your own map of a treasure island? To make it look like an old map, paint the paper with cold tea or coffee.

To make your map look even older, try drawing it using a fine black or brown felt-tip pen.

Crease the paper several times after drawing the map to make it look worn.

Make up spooky place names and write them on in old-fashioned looking writing.

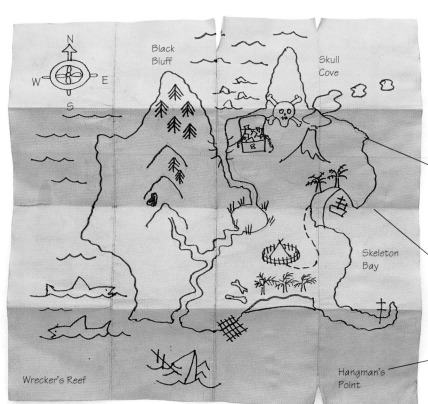

Spend a little time making sure that the roads and the coastline are in the right places, and then it will be much easier to fill in the rest of the map.

This map shows two different tree symbols. This one is for deciduous forest and the other is for coniferous forest.

Map symbols
Keep the symbols for the map very simple so that they can be understood at a glance. Make a note of them and try to use the same symbols on all the maps you make.

Map of Seatown

Sandy Hill

High Wood

Beach Road

Sea View Hotel

Beachy Brook

Swimmer's Cove

Key

Steep hill		Roads	
Farmland		Church	
River		Ice-cream Stand	
Sea		Café	
Sandy beach		Telephone booth	
Pebble beach		Mailbox	
Cliffs		Hotel	
Coniferous forest		Lighthouse	
Deciduous forest		Bus stop	
Footpath		Viewing point	

Color the sea and rivers blue.

Don't forget to draw where you stayed on your map.

NATURE MUSEUM

Good nature detectives keep their eyes open for new or interesting finds whenever they are outdoors. Unusual shells, pebbles, leaves, seed heads, stones, and twigs all make good collections to display. Here you can see how to make a tiny chest of drawers and a display showcase for your very own nature museum.

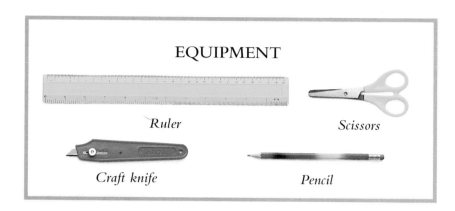

EQUIPMENT

Ruler

Scissors

Craft knife

Pencil

You will need

For the showcase

For the chest of drawers

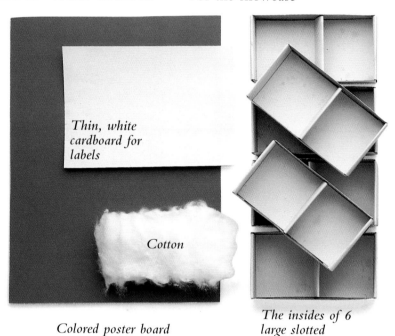

Thin, white cardboard for labels

Cotton

Colored poster board

The insides of 6 large slotted matchboxes★

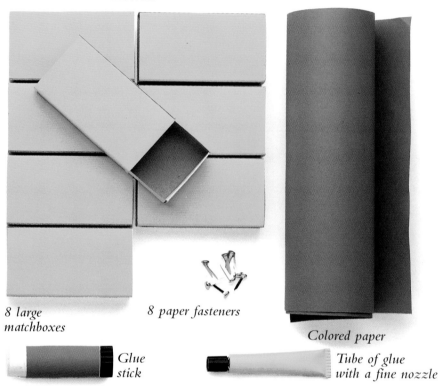

8 large matchboxes

8 paper fasteners

Colored paper

Glue stick

Tube of glue with a fine nozzle

Making the showcase

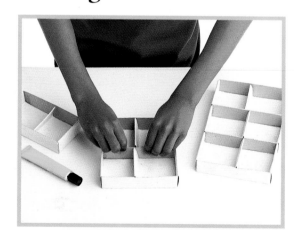

1 Glue three of the matchbox insides together, side by side in a row. Then glue three more box insides together in the same way.

2 Glue the two rows of three boxes together. Fold and glue down some of the cardboard slots in the boxes to make bigger drawers.

3 Ask an adult to cut a piece of poster board about 1 in (3 cm) bigger all around than the showcase. Then glue it onto the showcase.

★ *If you can't find slotted matchboxes, glue a small piece of cardboard in the middle of a single matchbox.*

Chest of drawers

1 Glue paper to the front ends of the matchbox insides and push a paper fastener through each one. Fold the dividers flat inside the boxes.

2 Glue two of the outer boxes together, side by side. Do this with all the outer boxes, then glue the pairs of boxes on top of each other.

3 Cut a strip of paper as wide as the length of the boxes and long enough to wrap around them. Glue the paper around the boxes.

Treasures on display

The tiny chest of drawers is a good place to keep nature treasures tucked away. Open the drawers a little if you want to display the contents. The showcase is for larger objects that you want to keep on display all the time.

Tiny shells

Tiny drawers
These tiny drawers are filled with miniature pebbles, seashells, and pieces of sea glass.

Showcase
You can use the showcase for any interesting finds, or keep it for one set collection, such as shells. Arrange the display to look as attractive as possible.

Line the bottom of each compartment with cotton.

Make labels from thin cardboard and glue them on.

New finds
Make your museum more interesting by changing the collection from time to time.

Sea glass in different colors, collected from the beach

Use the paper fasteners as drawer handles.

Rectangle of green paper glued to the front of the drawer

NATURE'S PICTURES

Even if you can't draw, you can create wonderful pictures based on things you find outdoors. Here you can learn how to make collages, pressed-flower pictures, bark rubbings, and paintings. Turn the page to see how to finish and frame the pictures.

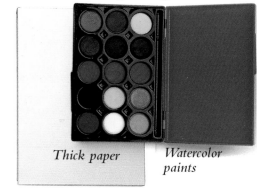

EQUIPMENT

Scissors *Ruler* *Jar of water*

Craft knife *Paintbrush*

Pencil

You will need

For pressed-flower and display pictures

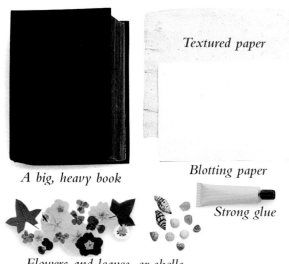

Textured paper

A big, heavy book *Blotting paper*

Strong glue

Flowers and leaves, or shells and sea glass

For frames

Masking tape *Colored poster board*

For tree collage

Textured paper *White glue* *Leaves, twigs, and sticks*

For bark rubbings

Masking tape

Wax crayons

Colored paper

For watercolor painting

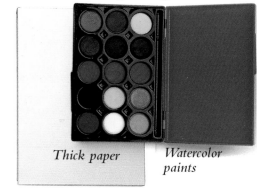

Thick paper *Watercolor paints*

For tissue-paper collage

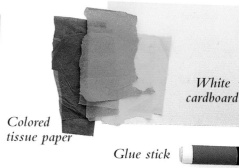

Colored tissue paper *White cardboard*

Glue stick

Pressing flowers

1 Open a big book and lay a sheet of blotting paper over it. Arrange the flowers flat on one half of the paper and fold the other half over them.

2 Press more flowers in the same way throughout the book. Close it and stack heavy books on top of it. Leave it for at least four weeks.

Flower picture

Arrange the pressed flowers on a sheet of paper. Then dab a tiny spot of glue on the back of each flower and gently stick it down in position.

Seashore picture

You can make a picture from a seashore collection. Arrange your treasures on a sheet of paper. Dab strong glue on the back of each item and stick it down.

Tree collage

1 To keep it firm, glue textured paper onto cardboard. Glue on a stick for the trunk, and twigs for the branches. Add leaves at the bottom.

2 Fill in the rest of the tree with clusters of fresh green leaves to look like the leaves of the tree. You may need to use a lot of glue.

Tissue-paper collage

1 Cut some strips of tissue paper to make the stems of flowers. Gently glue them to the paper and smooth out any wrinkles.

2 Tear petals out of tissue paper in different shades of yellow. Glue some of them down flat and others just at one end so they look ruffled.

Bark rubbings

1 Find a dry tree with fairly smooth bark and nothing growing on it. Tape a piece of paper firmly to the tree trunk.

2 Use the flat side of a wax crayon and rub it firmly up and down, to mark the bark pattern on the paper. Then untape the paper.

Flower painting

1 Put the flower you are painting in front of you and draw it as carefully as you can. Keep looking at the real flower to see what it is like.

2 Then paint the flower. Use one color at a time and let each color dry before painting the next so that they don't run together.

PICTURE GALLERY

Making a frame

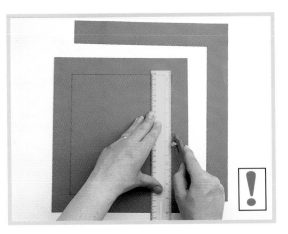

1 Measure the height and width of the picture. Add 1 in (3 cm) all the way around to give you the size of the outside of the rectangular frame.

2 Draw the outer frame on poster board, and then draw another rectangle inside this, each side 1½ in (4 cm) shorter than the outer frame.

3 To make the frame, ask an adult to cut along both the inner and outer rectangles for you, using a ruler and a craft knife.

Nature exhibition

Hang the finished pictures up in your room or beside your nature museum. Change your display through the year as the seasons change.

Daffodil pictures

Why not try using different techniques to make pictures of the same subject?

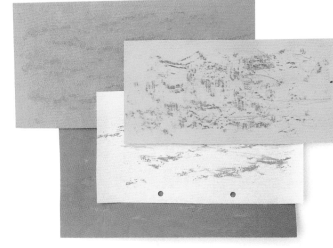

Bark rubbings

Try doing rubbings on different-colored papers, and use chalk as well as wax crayons to create different effects. Write the name of the tree the rubbing comes from on the back of the paper.

The loose petals on this tissue-paper collage give the flower a three-dimensional effect.

This picture of a daffodil in a blue pitcher was painted using watercolor paints.

4 Lay your picture facedown on the back of the frame, making sure the picture is centered, and then tape the picture to the frame.

Fresh leaves

Branches made from twigs

Dead leaves and twigs for the ground

Trunk made from a stick

Tree collage
Pictures like this are best displayed on a flat surface rather than hung up. The picture will last until the fresh leaves begin to wilt.

Shells

Sea glass

Shell collages
Collections like this work best if you keep the rows of objects simple and keep similar colors together. You could try arranging your shells into a shape instead.

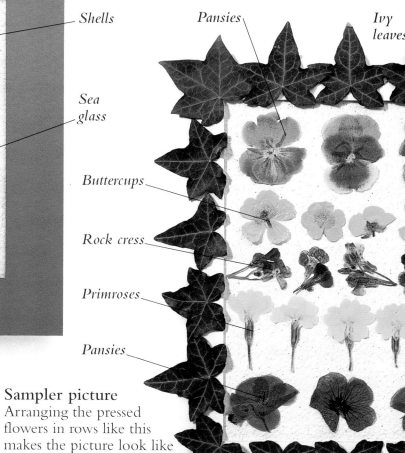

Pansies

Ivy leaves

Buttercups

Rock cress

Primroses

Pansies

Sampler picture
Arranging the pressed flowers in rows like this makes the picture look like a pretty and traditional needlework sampler.

WEATHER STATION

Is it going to be hot or cold today? Will it rain or will it be sunny? The weather changes all the time, but you can learn to spot signs of what it might do next. Here you can find out how to set up your own weather station and keep a record of the weather each day. Below you can see how to make a rain catcher and a wind vane. Turn the page to find out how to use them to keep a weather chart.

EQUIPMENT

Ruler

Small hammer

Scissors

Felt-tip pen

Craft knife

Pocket compass

You will need

For the wind vane

Tube of glue with a fine nozzle

Map pin

A dowel rod, 8 to 10 in (20 to 25 cm) long

A plastic container with a lid

A plastic drinking straw

Some stones or pebbles

Sand

Pieces of thin colored plastic, cut from containers

Tape in two different colors

For the rain catcher

A flat-bottomed clear plastic bottle

A drop of food coloring

A piece of thick cardboard or plastic

A dowel rod, 8 to 10 in (20 to 25 cm)

Modeling clay

Making the rain catcher

1 Cut off the bottom half of the bottle. Then cut off the funnel part of the top of the bottle. You will not need the middle section.

2 Slide the top part of the bottle upside down into the base of the bottle. It will act as a funnel. Stick the bottle edges together with tape.

3 Roll the modeling clay into a long strip and press it around the base of the rain catcher. Use this to hold the rain catcher in place outside.

4 Put a drop of food coloring into the bottle so that the rainwater you catch will be colored and you will be able to see it clearly.

5 To make a dipstick, put the dowel rod against a ruler. Use a felt-tip pen to make ½-in (1-cm) marks along half of the rod.

6 For decoration, wind tape around the top of the rod. Cut a cloud shape out of cardboard, color it, and tape it to the top of the rod.

Making the wind vane

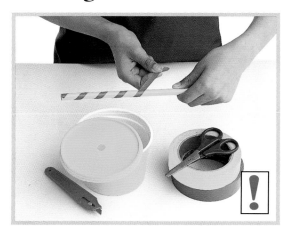

1 Make a hole in the lid of the plastic container with a craft knife. Wind tape, in two colors, around the dowel rod to decorate it.

2 Hold the rod upright in the center of the container and fill it with stones and sand. Slide the lid over the rod and press it on.

3 Cut four small triangles out of colored plastic. Then cut out two bigger triangles and two large "V" shapes, as shown in the picture.

4 Glue the four small triangles to the lid of the container in opposite pairs so that they are pointing in four different directions.

5 Glue the two large triangles together to cover one end of the straw. Glue the "V" shapes together to cover the other end of the straw.

6 Using a hammer, pin the straw to the top of the rod with the map pin so that the straw lies level and can spin freely in the wind.

WEATHER WATCH

Once you have made the rain catcher and wind vane, you will need to buy a simple thermometer to complete your weather station. Then draw up a weather chart and try to keep a daily record of the weather by studying the sky and using your instruments.

Weather chart

Make a weather chart by drawing a grid, like the one shown below, on some sheets of paper. Use paper fasteners to pin the grids onto a rectangle of stiff poster board. Draw the weather symbols you are going to use on a strip of paper and glue it along the bottom of the board.

Tape on a piece of ribbon to hang your chart.

Unfasten the top sheet of paper at the end of each week to give you a new chart for the next week.

Glue on a strip of paper and make a decorative heading.

Paper fasteners hold the grids in place on the poster board.

Weather Chart

Week beginning May 25	Sunday	Monday	Tuesday	Wednesday	Thursday	Friday	Saturday
Temperature	70°F (21°C)	64°F (18°C)	63°F (17°C)	63°F (17°C)	66°F (19°C)		
Wind direction	SW	SW	W	W	NW		
Rainfall	O	O	O	1/4 in	1/8 in		
Weather conditions							

Weather symbols	Clear sky	Partly cloudy	Cloudy	Windy	Lightning	Rain	Snow	Hail

Use these picture symbols, or make some up, to show what the weather is like.

You could add more symbols to show fog, mist, or frost.

Weather station

Set up your weather station outside and use the instruments to find out how much rain falls, what the temperature is, and which way the wind is blowing. Record your findings on your weather chart.

This thermometer shows the temperature in two scales, Celsius (°C) and Fahrenheit (°F).

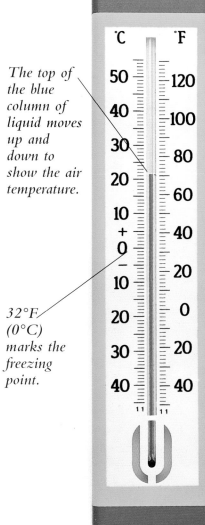

The top of the blue column of liquid moves up and down to show the air temperature.

32°F (0°C) marks the freezing point.

Rain catcher

Stand the rain catcher in an open space (without its dipstick). Fix it in place with the modeling clay and check every day to see whether there is any rainwater in it. If there is, dip the stick into it and measure the amount of water.

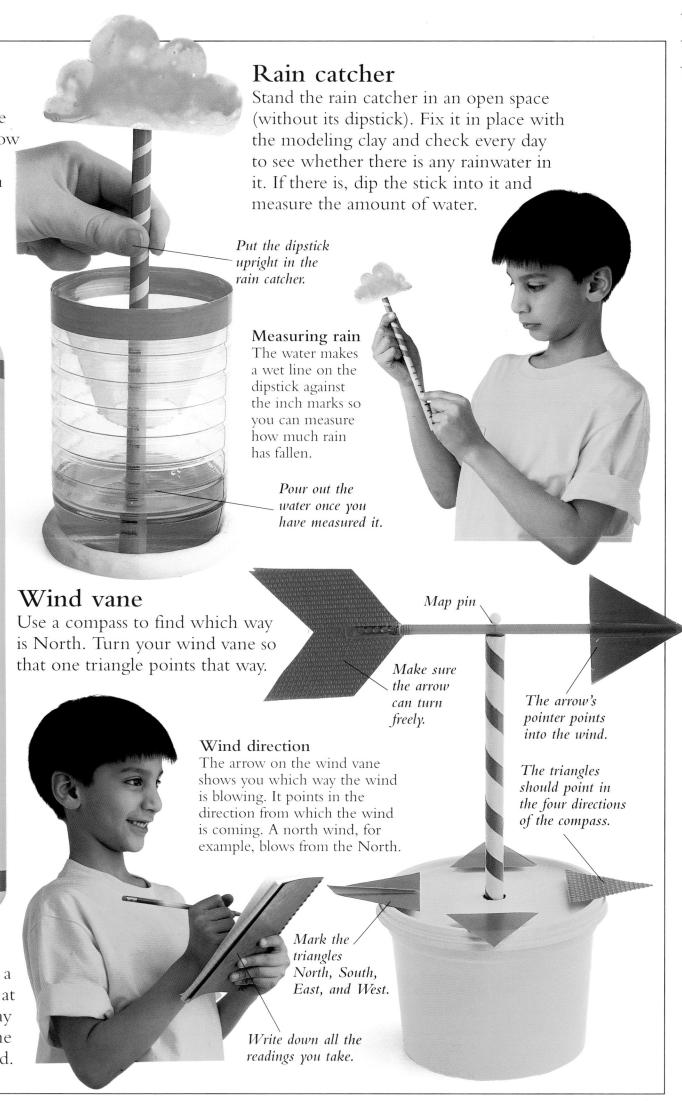

Put the dipstick upright in the rain catcher.

Measuring rain

The water makes a wet line on the dipstick against the inch marks so you can measure how much rain has fallen.

Pour out the water once you have measured it.

Wind vane

Use a compass to find which way is North. Turn your wind vane so that one triangle points that way.

Map pin

Make sure the arrow can turn freely.

The arrow's pointer points into the wind.

Wind direction

The arrow on the wind vane shows you which way the wind is blowing. It points in the direction from which the wind is coming. A north wind, for example, blows from the North.

The triangles should point in the four directions of the compass.

Mark the triangles North, South, East, and West.

Thermometer

Hang the thermometer in a shady place outside. Look at it at the same time each day and read the number by the top of the column of liquid.

Write down all the readings you take.

PLANT A GARDEN

You don't need much space to have a garden. Here and on the next page you can see how to plant a colorful garden of flowers and herbs on a plot that is only 3 ft (1 meter) square. For an instant garden, use mostly annual plants (colorful plants that last one summer). Below are some suggestions. Or sow seeds in trays in the spring, and plant them out in the garden during the early summer.

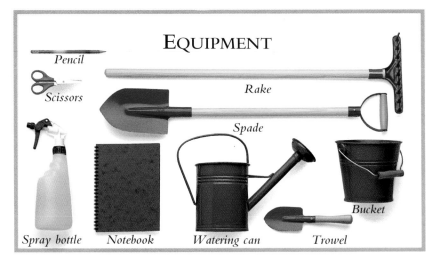

EQUIPMENT

Pencil

Scissors

Rake

Spade

Spray bottle   Notebook   Watering can   Trowel

Bucket

You will need

An attractive pot for the centerpiece

2 purple sage plants

2 variegated oregano plants

4 golden feverfew or golden marjoram plants

2 sweet basil plants

1 thyme plant

20 small, purple viola plants

2 pink-flowered strawberry plants

4 white marguerite plants

1 large, pink, perennial geranium plant

2 lilac petunia plants

4 large yellow viola plants

4 pink dianthus plants

Planting out

1 Decide where you are going to put a plant and dig a hole a little deeper than the plant's container. Check that the hole is big enough.

2 To take a plant out of a pot, tip the plant upside down between your fingers and squeeze the pot at the sides to loosen the soil.

3 Stand the plant in the hole you have dug. Fill in the spaces around it with soil and press the soil down. Then water the plant well.

Planning the garden

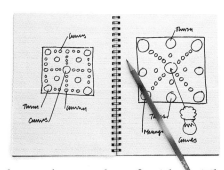

Look at other gardens for ideas. Then draw a plan based on a simple pattern and decide which plants to use.

Preparing the ground

First of all, working from the middle to the edges of the plot, take out the weeds (make sure that you remove all their roots, too). Dig over the ground to break up the soil. Then mix in some compost or potting soil to improve the ground. Finally, rake the soil level.

Arranging the plants

When you design your garden, always try to choose plants in colors that go well together.

1 Put the centerpiece in place, then plant the lines of plants that form the framework of your design.

2 Fill in the rest of the garden with plants. Allow enough space around each plant for it to grow.

GARDEN IN BLOOM

Once you have finished creating your garden, it is important to take care of the plants all year round. By following the steps below, you will have a healthy and long-lasting garden. Before buying any plants, check the labels to see what conditions they grow best in.

Watering

Water the plants every day, unless it rains, until they have settled in and started growing. After that, water them whenever the soil looks dry.

Pest control

Check the garden regularly for signs of pests. Remove snails, and spray aphids with a mixture of warm water and a bit of dishwashing liquid.

Deadheading

Plants will flower longer if you regularly pick or snip off the dead flower heads. Snip the herbs often to keep them small and bushy.

Gathering herbs

Once your herbs have grown, pick their leaves to cook with. If you used the pink-flowering strawberry plants, the fruit often tastes slightly bitter.

Spring bulbs

For a pretty spring garden, plant spring-flowering bulbs between the plants. Plant them in the fall following any instructions.

The finished garden

A white marguerite is planted at each corner.

Golden marjoram

Dianthus

Lilac and yellow viola

Pink-flowering strawberry plant

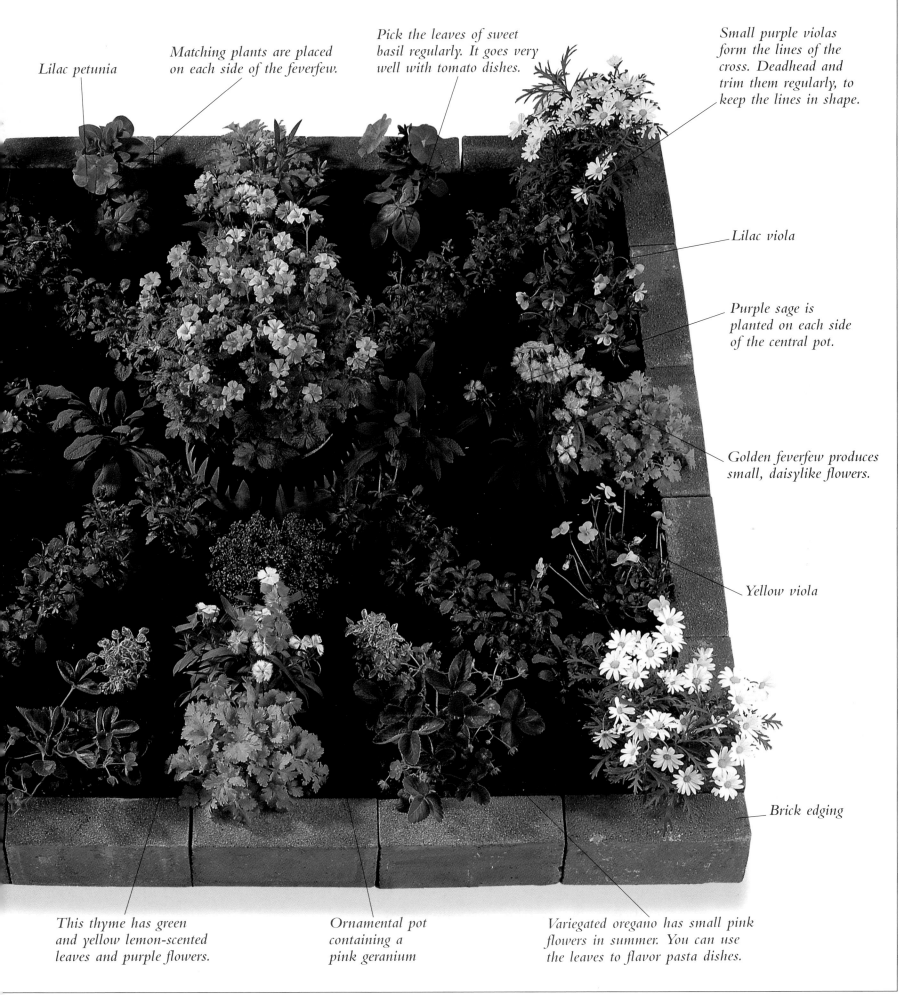

Lilac petunia

Matching plants are placed on each side of the feverfew.

Pick the leaves of sweet basil regularly. It goes very well with tomato dishes.

Small purple violas form the lines of the cross. Deadhead and trim them regularly, to keep the lines in shape.

Lilac viola

Purple sage is planted on each side of the central pot.

Golden feverfew produces small, daisylike flowers.

Yellow viola

Brick edging

This thyme has green and yellow lemon-scented leaves and purple flowers.

Ornamental pot containing a pink geranium

Variegated oregano has small pink flowers in summer. You can use the leaves to flavor pasta dishes.

GIANTS FROM SEEDS

Why not see if you can grow a giant plant from a tiny seed? Sunflowers and pumpkins can both grow to a huge size if they have the right conditions – and you are patient. Make sure you buy seed packets for the giant varieties. Then have a competition with a friend to see who can grow the tallest sunflower or the biggest pumpkin!

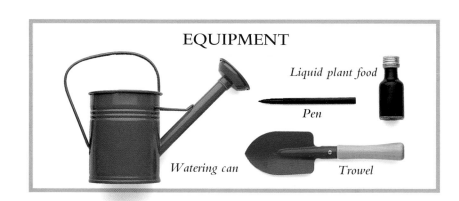

EQUIPMENT

Liquid plant food

Pen

Watering can

Trowel

You will need

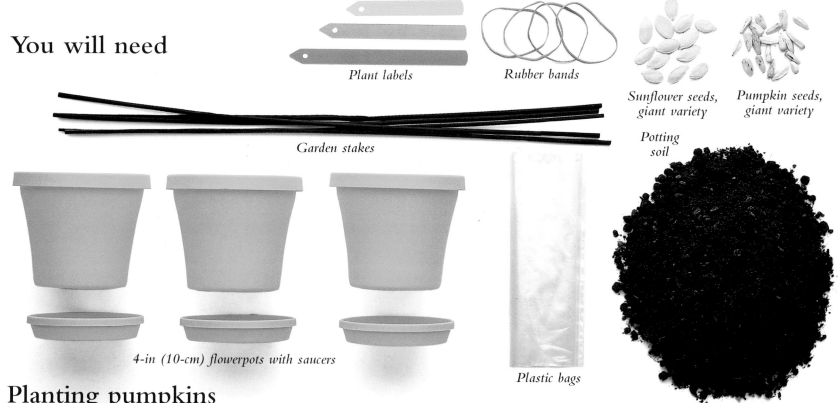

Plant labels

Rubber bands

Sunflower seeds, giant variety

Pumpkin seeds, giant variety

Garden stakes

Potting soil

4-in (10-cm) flowerpots with saucers

Plastic bags

Planting pumpkins

1 Fill the pots with soil and push two or three seeds about ³/₄ in (2 cm) into each one. Water well and label the seeds.

2 Secure plastic bags over the pots with a rubber band and place the pots on a light windowsill. When the first shoots appear, remove the bags.

3 After danger of frost is past, pull out all but the strongest seedling in each pot. Plant the strong seedlings in the garden and water them.

Sowing sunflowers

1 Plant three seeds where you want one plant, because they will not all grow. Push the seeds about ¼ in (1 cm) down into the soil.

2 Label the seeds and water them well. As the seedlings grow, pull out any weak ones, so the plants are about 1½ ft (45 cm) apart. Support small seedlings with stakes.

Golden giants

These pumpkins are trailing plants and will need at least 6 ft (two meters) each in which to grow. Harvest your pumpkins 12 to 20 weeks after they have been planted.

They are ripe when the skin hardens and the stem cracks. Cut them off their plants and stand in a warm bright place for 10 days, so the skin hardens further.

Mighty flowers

Sunflowers can grow up to 10 ft (3 meters) tall. To stop them from falling over, tie each sunflower to a stake as it grows taller. Measure the plants every week and keep a record of their heights in your nature logbook.

If you want a really tall plant, pinch out any side shoots as they appear. When the seeds are ripe, cut off the sunflower heads, keep the seeds, and save them for planting the following year.

Once the skin has hardened, use your pumpkin for cooking, or scoop out the inside and use the hollow shell as a candle holder.

BIRD FEEDERS

The best way to find out about birds is to put out food for them so that you can watch them from nearby. Here and on the next pages you can find out how to make traditional bird feeders, some nifty hanging feeders, and gourmet bird pudding. You will need an adult's help to make the bird feeders.

You will need

For the bird feeders

4 tray sides, 1-in (2-cm) softwood

2 of each length

9¹/₂ in (24.5 cm) long x 1 in (2 cm) wide

6¹/₂ in (17 cm) long x 1 in (2 cm) wide

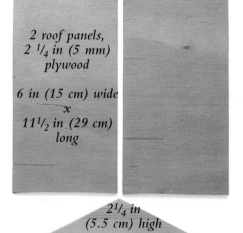

Tray base, ¹/₄-in (5-mm) plywood

10 in (25 cm) wide x 10 in (25 cm) long

2 roof gables, 1-in (2-cm) softwood

2 roof panels, 2 ¹/₄ in (5 mm) plywood

6 in (15 cm) wide x 11¹/₂ in (29 cm) long

2¹/₄ in (5.5 cm) high

8¹/₄ in (21.5 cm) long

Strong wooden post, 5 ft (1.5 m) long

2 roof panels, 2¹/₄-in (5-mm) plywood

8¹/₂ in (21.5 cm) long x 3 in (7.5 cm) wide

4 screw hooks

A 2-in (5-cm) nail

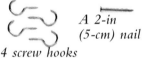

1-in (2-cm) nails

Wood sealant

For the bird feeders

Small hammer

Ruler

Large hammer

Paintbrush

Tape

Scissors

Pencil

Craft knife

For the bird feed

Small saucepan

Large needle

Wooden spoon

Bowl

For bird pudding feeders

Oats

Birdseed

Cooked vegetables

Dried fruit

Large pinecone

Cooked rice

Bread crumbs

Nuts (not salted)

²/₃ cup (100 g) lard

Small yogurt container

Forked twig

For the carton feeder

Small milk carton

For the peanut feeder

Peanuts in their shells

Garden twine

Open bird feeder

1 Tape the two longer tray sides to opposite sides of the tray base. Tape the two shorter sides in place, leaving gaps at the corners.

2 Turn the tray over. Nail the base of the tray to the tray sides with 1-in (2-cm) nails, using a small hammer.★ Then peel off the tape.

Bird feeder with roof

3 Draw diagonal lines across the tray to find the center. Ask an adult to nail the tray to the post with a 2-in (5-cm) nail where the lines cross.

4 Screw two hooks into each of the longer sides of the tray. Then ask an adult to set up the bird feeder in the garden (see page 45).

1 Follow steps 1 and 2 for the open bird feeder. Then measure and draw a pencil line ¾ in (2 cm) in from each side of the two roof pieces.

2 Rest the roof gables on blocks of wood. Nail the roof panels onto the gables, lining up the gables inside the pencil lines you have drawn.

3 Hold the roof against a table. Nail one of the roof supports to the center of a gable with 1-in (2-cm) nails. Do the same on the other side.

4 Stand the tray and roof on their sides. Nail the roof supports to the outer edges of the short tray sides. Then nail the tray to the post.★

Bird pudding feeder

1 Melt the lard in a saucepan over low heat. Put all of the food in a bowl and pour the melted lard over it. Mix it in well.

2 Spoon the pudding mixture into the yogurt container. Push the twig into the mixture, then leave the pudding until it sets.

3 When the pudding has set, pull it out of the yogurt container by the twig and roll it in birdseed. Tie a piece of string to the twig.

*Ask an adult to do this as in Step 3 for the Open bird feeder..

BIRD WATCH

Peanut feeder

Thread a big needle with a double length of garden twine. Knot the ends of the twine together, then thread the peanuts onto it.

Milk carton feeder

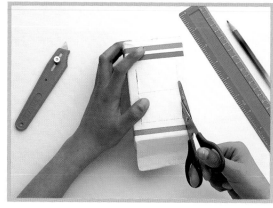

1 Draw a rectangle, with a line across it a third of the way up, on the front of the carton. Cut along the sides and top of the rectangle.

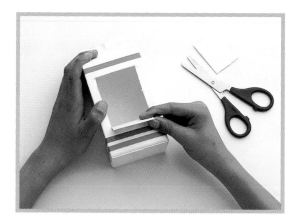

2 Cut along the middle line and bend back the flap along the bottom line of the rectangle. Do the same on the back of the carton.

Bird patrol

The more you watch birds, the easier it will become to recognize common ones. Find out which birds live in and visit your local area first, then try bird watching in woods, by a river, or by the sea. It helps to make quick sketches. Look for a bird's color, size, the shape of its beak, wings, and feet, and any special features.

Draw ovals for the body and head.

Add the beak and tail.

Then fill in the wings and feet.

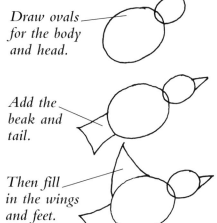

Lying low

If you are bird watching, it is very important to lie still and keep quiet so that you do not frighten away the birds. You could make a blind and watch from there (see page 8).

What was it?

If you don't recognize a bird, draw a sketch of it and make some notes to help you look it up in a field guide at home.

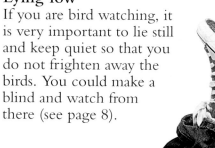

A closer look

It is a good idea to carry binoculars with you so that you can look closely at any birds you see.

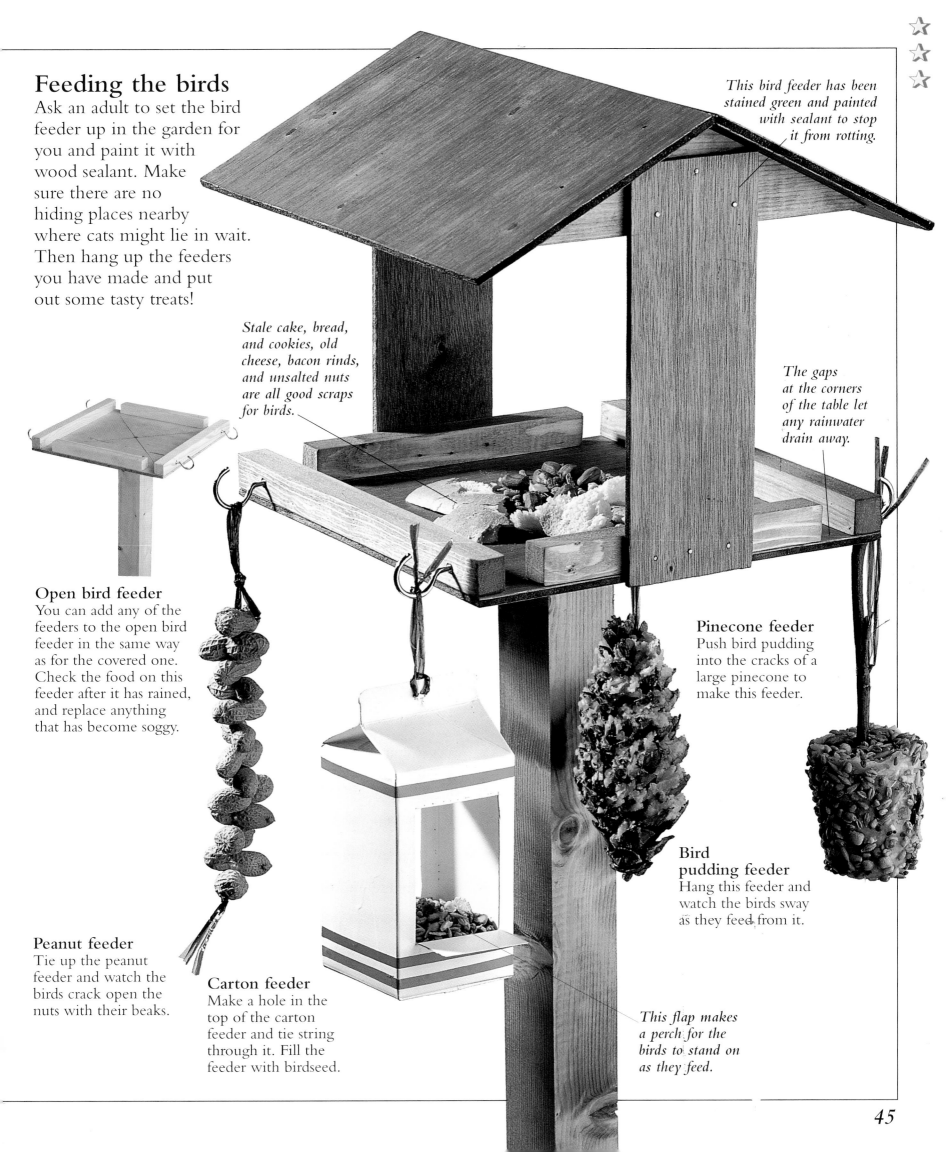

Feeding the birds

Ask an adult to set the bird feeder up in the garden for you and paint it with wood sealant. Make sure there are no hiding places nearby where cats might lie in wait. Then hang up the feeders you have made and put out some tasty treats!

This bird feeder has been stained green and painted with sealant to stop it from rotting.

Stale cake, bread, and cookies, old cheese, bacon rinds, and unsalted nuts are all good scraps for birds.

The gaps at the corners of the table let any rainwater drain away.

Open bird feeder
You can add any of the feeders to the open bird feeder in the same way as for the covered one. Check the food on this feeder after it has rained, and replace anything that has become soggy.

Pinecone feeder
Push bird pudding into the cracks of a large pinecone to make this feeder.

Bird pudding feeder
Hang this feeder and watch the birds sway as they feed from it.

Peanut feeder
Tie up the peanut feeder and watch the birds crack open the nuts with their beaks.

Carton feeder
Make a hole in the top of the carton feeder and tie string through it. Fill the feeder with birdseed.

This flap makes a perch for the birds to stand on as they feed.

IN CLOSE-UP

All around you, on the ground, in the water, and in the air, tiny creatures are busily leading their own lives. To find out more about these mini-beasts, you will need to collect some and take a closer look. Here and on the next page you can find out how to make four useful pieces of equipment: a collecting jar, a water viewer, a fishing net, and an amazing insect catcher.

Here and on the next page

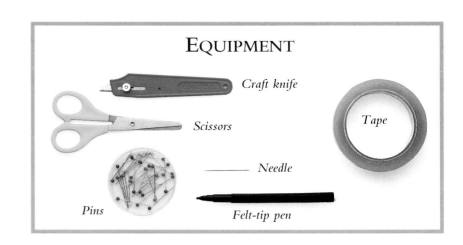

EQUIPMENT

Craft knife

Scissors

Tape

Needle

Pins

Felt-tip pen

You will need

For the fishing net

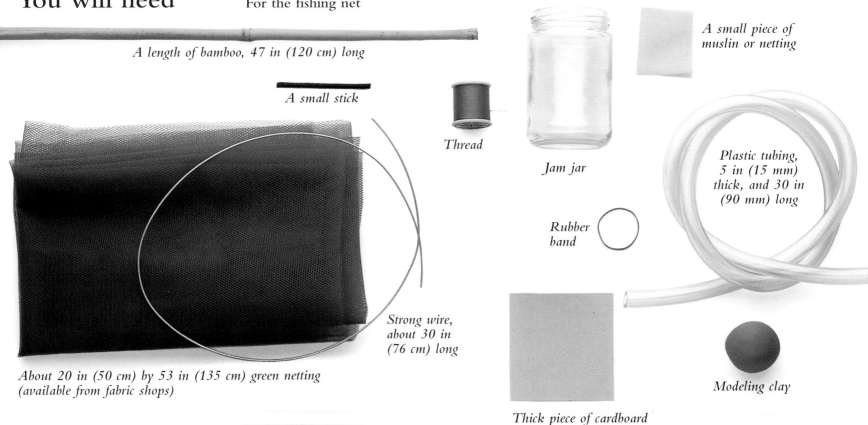

A length of bamboo, 47 in (120 cm) long

A small stick

Thread

Jam jar

For the insect catcher

A small piece of muslin or netting

Plastic tubing, 5 in (15 mm) thick, and 30 in (90 mm) long

Rubber band

Strong wire, about 30 in (76 cm) long

About 20 in (50 cm) by 53 in (135 cm) green netting (available from fabric shops)

Thick piece of cardboard

Modeling clay

For the water viewer

Rubber band

Large plastic yogurt container

Plastic wrap

For the collecting jar

Piece of muslin or netting

Jam jar

Rubber band

String

Collecting jar

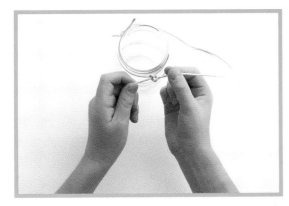

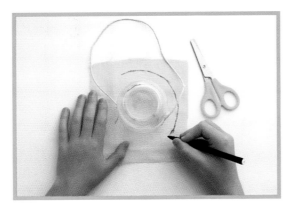

1 Tie a long piece of string around the neck of the jar, leaving a long end free. Tie the free end across the jar to make a handle as shown.

2 Stand the jar on a piece of muslin. With a felt-tip pen, draw a circle about 1 in (2 cm) bigger than the base of the jar around it.

3 Cut out the circle of muslin. Lay it on top of the jar and stretch it flat. Then fasten it in place around the neck of the jar with a rubber band.

Fishing net

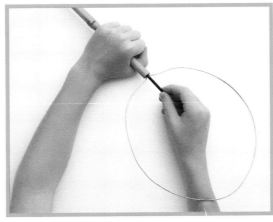

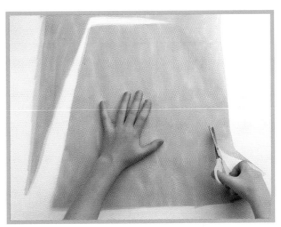

1 Bend the piece of wire into a circle, then bend the wire out about 1½ in (4 cm) from each end, as shown, to form two prongs.

2 Push the two prongs of the wire circle into the end of the bamboo pole. Push a small stick into the pole to wedge the wire in place.

3 Fold the netting in half. Cut out two pieces 14 in (36 cm) deep, 14½ in (37 cm) wide at the top, and 9½ in (24 cm) wide at the bottom.

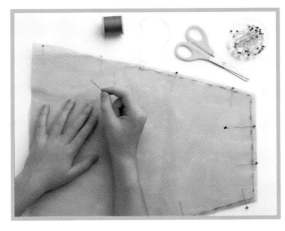

4 Pin the pieces of netting together around three sides, leaving the top open. Sew along the pinned sides, ½ in (1 cm) in from the edges.★

5 Remove the pins and turn the netting inside out to form your net. Fold the top of it over the wire circle and pin it in place.

6 Sew the net firmly around the wire, starting and finishing with double stitches★ next to the pole. Finally, remove the pins.

★*Ask an adult to help you with this.*

MINI-BEAST PATROL

Water viewer

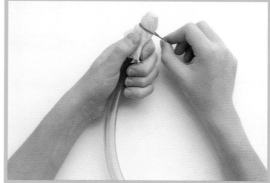

1 Ask an adult to cut out the bottom of the yogurt container very carefully, using a craft knife. Do not try to do this yourself.

2 Cut out a large circle of plastic wrap. Stretch it over the top of the yogurt container and fasten it tightly in place with a rubber band.

Insect catcher

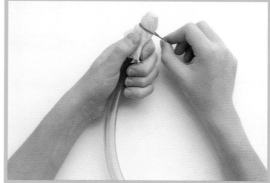

1 Draw a circle around the top of the jam jar on cardboard. Inside this, draw two smaller circles around the tubing. Cut out the circles.

2 Cut the tubing into two pieces 10 in (25 cm) long and 20 in (50 cm) long. Fix muslin over one end of the short tube with a rubber band.

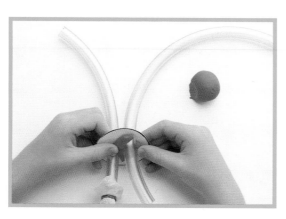

3 Push the two pieces of tubing through the holes in the cardboard circle. Wedge them both in place underneath with modeling clay.

4 Fasten the circle of cardboard to the top of the jar with tape, then press modeling clay over the top of the the tube circles to hold them in place.

Bug watch

Take your fishing net, collecting jar, water viewer, and insect catcher to different habitats, such as meadows, woods, ponds, or the seashore, to look for mini-wildlife. It is a good idea to take a magnifying glass, notebook, and pencil with you, too.

Kindness, not cruelty

Remember – mini-beasts are living creatures, so treat them kindly. Only keep them for as long as you have to, study them and make notes, then gently put them back where you found them. Always wash your hands after touching pond water, animals, and soil.

Suck in air through the end of this tube.

Remove the muslin cover to put an insect in the jar, then fasten the cover on again.

Collecting jar

String handle

Examining mini-beasts

You can use the collecting jar to examine creatures you find on land, such as this spider. You can also use it to house water creatures you catch with the fishing net. However, you must fill the jar with water from where you are fishing so that the water creatures can breathe.

Viewing end

Water sight
The edges of ponds, streams, and tide pools are all good places to look for mini-beasts, but be very careful on slippery banks and rocks, and make sure there is an adult with you at all times. To use the water viewer, dip the plastic-covered end a few inches into the water and look through the hole. You should get a good view of life below the surface of the water.

Fishing net

Bamboo handle

Net

Plastic wrap screen

Water viewer

Wire circle

What have I found?
Study each creature you find. What is it doing? Can you see the creature's head? Does it have eyes or antennae? How many legs and wings has it got, and how many parts to its body? Do a quick sketch of each creature you find.

Underwater search
Use your fishing net in ponds, streams, or tide pools. Try sweeping it over the surface of the water to see what you find, then try collecting lower down. You could also try scooping up mud and stones from the bottom, but take care not to rip your net. Do you find different mini-beasts at each level?

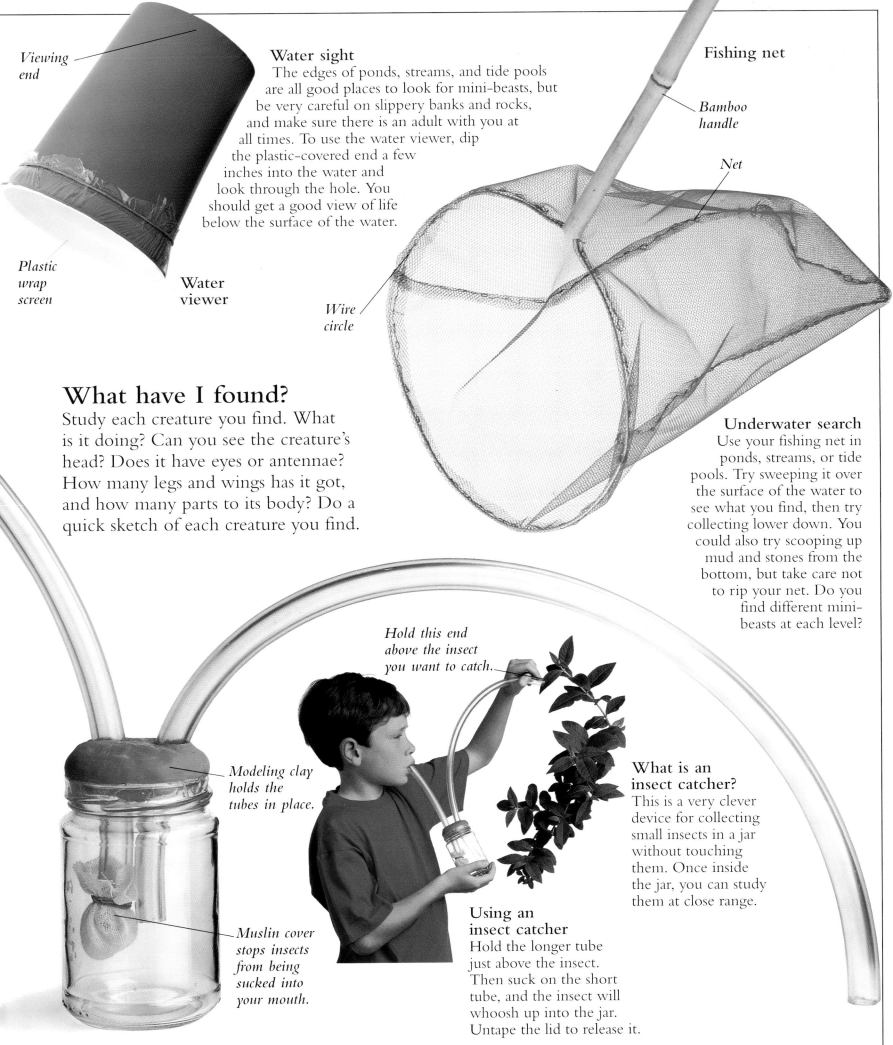

Hold this end above the insect you want to catch.

Modeling clay holds the tubes in place.

What is an insect catcher?
This is a very clever device for collecting small insects in a jar without touching them. Once inside the jar, you can study them at close range.

Muslin cover stops insects from being sucked into your mouth.

Using an insect catcher
Hold the longer tube just above the insect. Then suck on the short tube, and the insect will whoosh up into the jar. Untape the lid to release it.

NATURE LOGBOOK

Your nature logbook is your own record of all the things you see, find, and collect on your expeditions outdoors. You can draw in it, stick in unusual treasures, put in pressed plants, magazine clippings, and photographs you have taken, and keep records of surveys or experiments you have done. To make your logbook really special, why not make the book yourself with different sorts of cardboard and paper? You can see how below.

The cover
Stick a picture on the cover and add a torn paper square for the title.

Roughly knot the raffia to give the book a natural look.

Sam's Nature Logbook

Choose a stick slightly longer than the height of the book.

Draw a picture to stick on the front cover of your book.

EQUIPMENT

Ruler

Scissors

Hole punch

Pencil

Making the logbook

Cut two rectangles of poster board for the cover. For the pages, cut paper into slightly smaller rectangles. Punch holes through all the sheets.

You will need

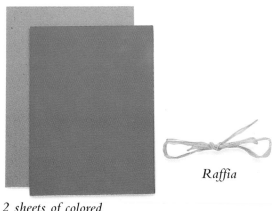

Raffia

2 sheets of colored poster board

A variety of sheets of paper and tracing paper

A straight stick

2 Put the paper inside the covers, lining up the holes. Tie pieces of raffia through the holes and around the stick to hold the book together.

Expedition notebook
The notes you make in your expedition notebook will provide lots of material for your logbook. Copy things out, giving details of the dates and places.

Collections
Things you have collected can be taped and glued into your log book.

Pages made with paper of different textures and colours, make the log book look interesting.

Catkins

Pussy willow

Flowers found in Grandma's garden

Bird table survey

Food		Mon	Tue	Wed	Thur	Fri
Apple		2	3			
Seed feeder		6	4			
Bird pudding		3	4			
Breadcrumbs		15				
Cheese		4				

Song thrush seen in Grandma's garden on Sunday

Speckled breast

Giant daisy

Aubretia

Pansies

Buttercups

Plastic envelope of seeds collected

Bird study
Copy any sketches you make outdoors (see page 44), filling in as much detail and colour as you can from your notes.

Collect pictures of birds and insects.

Small flower press to take on expeditions

Plant file
Your nature log book is a good place to keep pressed flowers and leaves (see page 28)★. Stick them in gently with glue and cover them with a sheet of tracing paper to protect them.

★*Remember – never pick or uproot wild plants.*

MAKE A KITE

Why not make your own kite with a tail and paint it bold colors to stand out against the sky? The kite is made of thin plastic, so keep an eye out for a large, brightly colored plastic bag with no writing on it. To decorate the kite you will need acrylic paints or felt-tip pens. Turn the page to see how to finish the kite and send it flying!

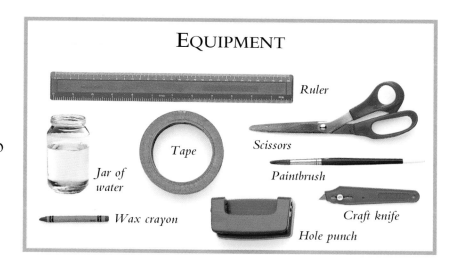

EQUIPMENT

Ruler

Scissors

Tape

Paintbrush

Jar of water

Wax crayon

Hole punch

Craft knife

You will need

A large plastic bag

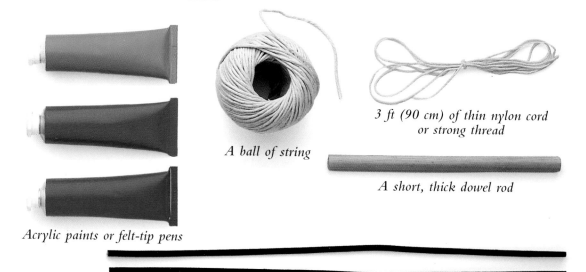

Acrylic paints or felt-tip pens

A ball of string

3 ft (90 cm) of thin nylon cord or strong thread

A short, thick dowel rod

2 garden stakes, 1½ ft (46 cm) long

What to do

1 Cut out a square of plastic 19 in (48 cm) wide. Mark the center top and bottom and make three marks, in a line, 5½ in (14 cm) from the top.

2 Draw straight lines to join up the marks at the edges of the plastic square. Cut carefully along the lines, keeping the plastic flat.

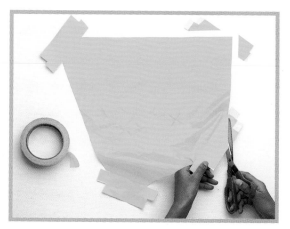

3 Stick two strips of tape across all the corners of the kite, both back and front, to strengthen them. Trim the pieces of tape to fit the corners.

4 Fold over each corner of the kite in turn and punch a hole through the double thickness to make two holes next to each other, as shown.

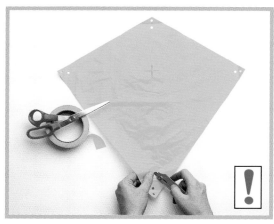

5 Stick tape to the center of the kite 4 in (11 cm) from the top and 2³⁄₄ in (7 cm) from the bottom. Ask an adult to cut a slit in the tape.

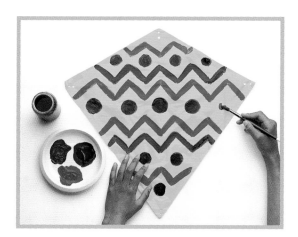

6 Paint the front of the kite with acrylic paints to decorate it. Keep your design bold and simple and do not let the colors run. Leave the kite to dry.

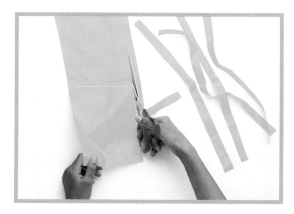

7 Cut about eight ribbons of thin plastic all the same length. Hold the ribbons together and punch a hole through one end of them.

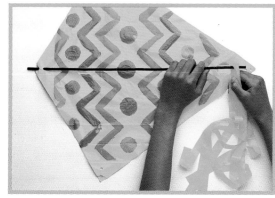

8 Push the end of one stake through the holes in the top of the kite. Thread the kite tail ribbons onto the other end of the stake

9 Tape the top end of the stake in place. Push the other end of the stake through the holes at the bottom of the kite and tape that in place, too.

10 Push the ends of the second stake through the side holes in the kite. Tape it in place in the same way, pulling the plastic tight.

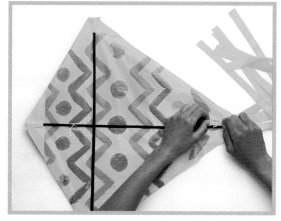

11 Thread the ends of the cord through the slits in the kite from the painted side. Knot each end onto the stake at the back of the kite.

12 Turn the kite over and tie a small loop in the cord. The loop should be directly over the top slit when you pull the cord up tight.

FLYING HIGH

Making the handle

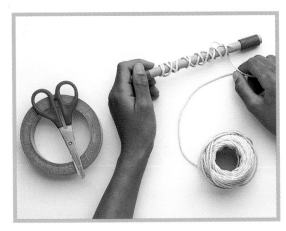

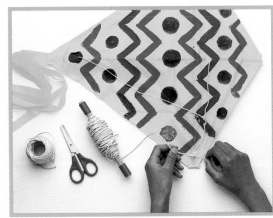

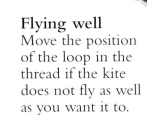

1 Wrap tape around each end of the dowel rod. Tie one end of the ball of string to the rod, then wind on about 100 ft (30 meters) of string.

2 Tie the loose end of the string through the loop in the thread at the front of the kite. Knot it twice to make sure it is secure.

Flying well
Move the position of the loop in the thread if the kite does not fly as well as you want it to.

Flying the kite

Wait for a windy day to fly your kite, then look for an open space, away from any trees, buildings, overhead wires, or roads. Ask a friend to go with you to help you launch the kite.

Crash landings
If the kite dives and crashes, rewind most of the string before you try to launch it again.

Launching the kite
Stand with your back to the wind and unwind a few feet of the kite string. Ask your friend to carry the kite away from you, holding it up into the wind. Then have them toss the kite up into the air. As it goes up, start letting out more string.

Keep pulling on the string to keep it tight and the kite should rise into the air.

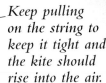

Hold the rod at each end and keep it straight to help you control the kite.

Kite designs

You could decorate your kite with a sun, a giant butterfly pattern, or any designs of your own. You could also make a multicolored tail for it.

The looped thread is always at the front of the kite.

Kite tails
If the kite keeps nose-diving, try making a longer tail for it.

The kite tail helps keep it steady in the air.

Make sure the plastic is stretched tightly against the stakes on the back of it, keeping the kite firm.

TINY BOATS

You may know a pond, a bubbling stream, or a tide pool that would be good for sailing model boats. If so, try out your boat-building skills and make a boat that really sails in the wind. Below you can find out how to make a mini-raft and a colorful catamaran from odds and ends you can find around your home or yard. Ask an adult to go with you when you play near water.

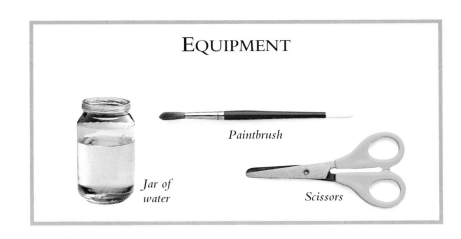

EQUIPMENT

Jar of water

Paintbrush

Scissors

You will need

For the raft

Small, stright sticks about the same length

Raffia

Modeling clay

For the catamaran

3 thread spools

4 champagne or wine corks

2 bendy plastic drinking straws

Poster paint

Tube of strong glue

Ice pop sticks

For sails for both boats

Colored paper

A glue stick

Making the raft

1 Cut out a square of paper for the sail. Cut two slits in the paper, as shown, and thread a stick through them. Glue a paper sun onto the sail.

2 Put eight sticks of the same length next to each other and lay a stick across each end. Tie the sticks tightly together with pieces of raffia.

3 Push one end of the stick mast into a lump of modeling clay. Then push the modeling clay firmly in place on the middle of the raft.

Making the catamaran

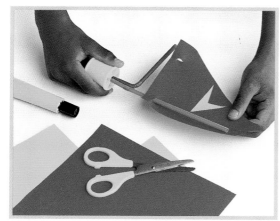

1 Cut out a triangle of paper for the sail and make a slit in each corner. Push two straws into a spool and thread them onto the sail as shown.

2 Paint three ice pop sticks and let them dry. Then glue them across two spools. Glue the spool and sail to the middle of the sticks.

3 Glue the flat ends of the corks onto the ends of the spools. Then make a flag with the bent end of a straw and push it onto the mast.

Setting sail

Place the boats gently on the water and see how they float. The catamaran will float best if the mast is stuck right in the center of the ice pop sticks. Turn the boats until the sails catch the wind and see which one goes fastest!

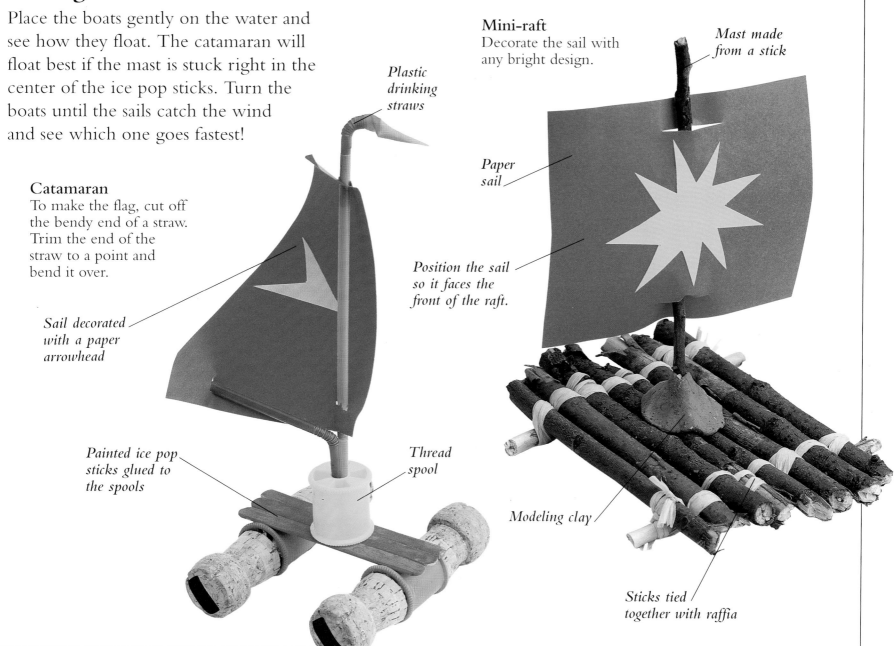

Mini-raft
Decorate the sail with any bright design.

Mast made from a stick

Plastic drinking straws

Paper sail

Catamaran
To make the flag, cut off the bendy end of a straw. Trim the end of the straw to a point and bend it over.

Position the sail so it faces the front of the raft.

Sail decorated with a paper arrowhead

Painted ice pop sticks glued to the spools

Thread spool

Modeling clay

Sticks tied together with raffia

NATURE'S MODELS

On a quiet afternoon, why not try making a model with some of the things you have collected outdoors? With a little imagination you can transform twigs, leaves, and feathers into works of art. Here and on the next page you can find out how to create tiny mice, a corn doll, a wooden seagull, and a sunflower.

You will need

For the corn doll

Thick thread

Evergreen leaves

Raffia or long pieces of straw

For the sunflower

Bundle of small, straight twigs

Small pinecones

A piece of strong cardboard

For the seagull

2 matching rectangles of flat wood for the body

Pieces of wood for the head, neck, and beak

Flat piece of wood for the base

Shell

A thin, straight stick

Evergreen leaves

Gray or white feathers

Two long, thin twigs

For the mice

Pink paper

A medium-sized pinecone for each mouse

Raffia

Small pieces of sea glass or small shells

Corn doll

1 Cut at least 25 pieces of raffia about 10 in (25 cm) long. Tie them together in the middle with thick thread to make the doll's waist.

2 Divide the raffia in half below the waist to make two legs. Tie thread around each leg at the top, in the middle, and near the bottom.

3 Tie thread around the doll's chest and split the raffia above it into three sections. Tie the two outer sections, as shown, to make arms.

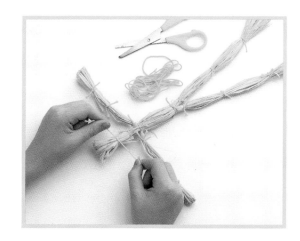

4 Tie thread around the raffia just above the arms to make a neck. Then fold back the raffia and tie it at the neck, as shown, to make the head.

5 Wind pieces of raffia around the doll's body and neck to make them look fatter, then tie the ends and tuck them into the doll's body.

6 Make a dress by tying leaves to the doll's waist with a piece of raffia. Make a hat out of small leaves and attach it to her head.

Seagull sculpture

1 Glue two twigs to one of the matching rectangles of wood for legs. Glue on two tail feathers and add a small piece of wood for a neck.

2 Glue the other matching wooden rectangle in place over the first to cover the places where the legs, neck, and tail feathers join the body.

3 Glue a thin piece of wood to the back of the neck for the lower beak. Glue a larger piece of wood to the front of the neck for the head.

4 Glue two feathers to each side of the bird's body for wings, so that the back set of feathers points upward and the front set points downward.

5 Glue a small shell to the bird's head to make an eye. Draw a small black circle on the shell to make the pupil of the eye.

6 Let the glue dry, then glue the bird's legs into a flat piece of wood to make a stand. (Ask an adult to make two holes in the wood for you.)

NATURE GALLERY

Sunflower on a stick

1 Cut a circle out of a thick piece of cardboard. Glue pinecones over the circle to make the center of the flower. Leave the glue to dry.

2 Turn the circle of cardboard over. Glue short, straight twigs and large leaves alternately to the back of the circle to form the petals.

3 Glue a long, straight stick to the bottom of the cardboard circle. Let the glue dry completely before turning the sunflower over.

On display

The models you make will vary depending on the materials you have at hand, but that just makes them more interesting. Use the models here as starting points for your own ideas.

Corn doll

You can dress your corn doll with any natural materials you can find. Look for things like seed heads, twigs, bark, and dried flowers.

Large evergreen leaf

Short, straight twig

Arrange the pinecones in a pattern on the cardboard.

Long, straight twig stem

Sunflower on a stick
When the evergreen leaves begin to droop, replace them with more leaves or with petals made of yellow paper.

Hat made from small leaves

Raffia arm

Raffia belt holding the dress in place

Dress of evergreen leaves

Pinecone mice

1 Glue two small pieces of sea glass or shells to the front of the cone under the open end. These are feet for the cones to balance on.

2 Cut two small ears out of pink paper and fold them in the middle. Glue them in place near the top of the pinecone for ears.

3 Glue on two tiny pieces of sea glass for eyes below the ears. Cut short pieces of raffia for the tail and whiskers and glue them in place.

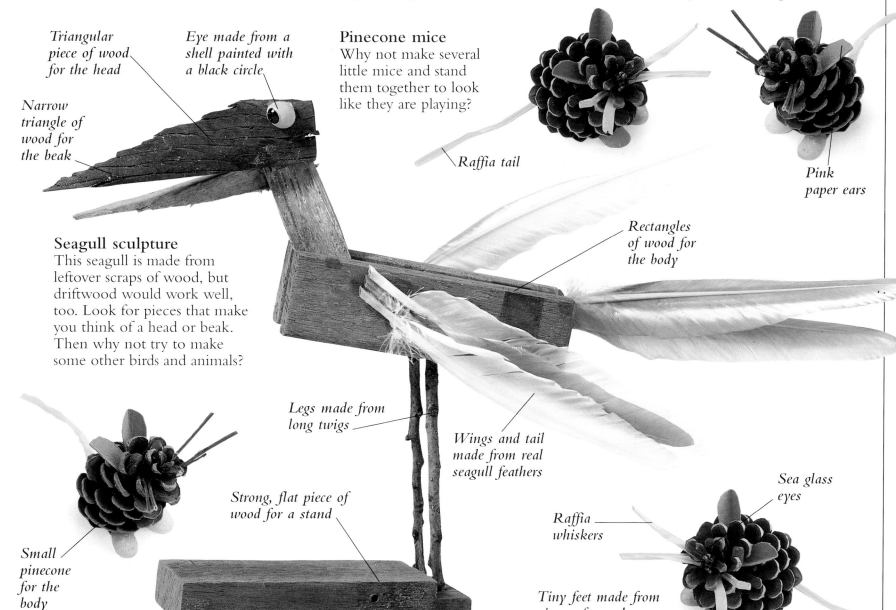

Triangular piece of wood for the head

Eye made from a shell painted with a black circle

Pinecone mice
Why not make several little mice and stand them together to look like they are playing?

Narrow triangle of wood for the beak

Raffia tail

Pink paper ears

Rectangles of wood for the body

Seagull sculpture
This seagull is made from leftover scraps of wood, but driftwood would work well, too. Look for pieces that make you think of a head or beak. Then why not try to make some other birds and animals?

Legs made from long twigs

Wings and tail made from real seagull feathers

Sea glass eyes

Raffia whiskers

Small pinecone for the body

Strong, flat piece of wood for a stand

Tiny feet made from pieces of sea glass

HANDY HINTS

This picture guide illustrates skills you will find helpful with some of the projects in this book. If you want to practice your reef knots, use different-colored ropes or strings as in the steps below.

Using a compass

1 Hold the compass steady in your hand and away from anything metal. Then wait until the colored end of the needle stops moving.

2 Turn the compass around until the colored end of the needle lines up with the symbol for North. You are now facing magnetic North.

Hammering in a nail

1 Using a ruler and pencil, make a mark on the exact positions where you want the nails to go into the piece of wood.

2 Hold the nail about halfway down and place it on a pencil mark. Give it a firm tap with the hammer to drive it into the wood.

3 Remove your hand and, holding the hammer near the end, hit the nail squarely until its head lies on the surface of the wood.

Tying a reef knot

1 Hold the ends of two pieces of rope or string in each hand. Wrap the end of the green rope over and then under the end of the yellow rope.

2 Now take the free end of the green rope and place it over and then across the end of the yellow rope.

3 Finally, wrap the green rope around the yellow rope and up through the hole in the middle. Then pull both ends of rope tightly.

OUTDOOR CODE

Whatever you are doing outside, whether going for a walk or arranging a nature expedition, plan your activities sensibly and respect the countryside and its wildlife. Here are some important points to remember.

•

Always tell your parents or guardians where you are going and what you plan to do.

•

Before setting off, make sure you are wearing suitable clothes, have any equipment or food you need, and have change for a phone call home.

•

Do not litter. Take any garbage home with you.

•

Stick to paths and trails and fasten all gates behind you.

•

Always leave things as you found them. Do not damage any plants or trees.

•

When collecting things in the wild, only take what you need and make sure you leave plenty of specimens behind.

•

Only pick wildflowers if there are plenty growing, and just pick a few. Never pick rare plants or uproot any plant.

•

Never disturb nesting birds or take birds' eggs

•

Be gentle with any creatures you catch. Study them gently and make notes quickly, then put them back where you found them.

INDEX